THE WOODHEAD ROUTE

Anthony Dawson

AMBERLEY

Acknowledgements

I should like to thank Mr Adrian Bailey, a fellow railway volunteer at MOSI, for his time and enthusiasm in recalling his days working on the Woodhead Line. It is to him and all those who worked on the Woodhead that this book is most respectfully dedicated.

In preparation of the manuscript I would also like to thank Andy Mason for journeying along the Woodhead with me, members of the Woodhead Railway Heritage Group, and the MOSI Railway team for their continued friendship and encouragement.

All photographs and images are by the author/from the author's collection unless otherwise stated.

Abbreviations:

GC	Great Central Railway.
L&M	Liverpool & Manchester Railway.
LNWR	London & North Western Railway.
M&B	Manchester & Birmingham Railway.
M&L	Manchester & Leeds Railway.
MS&L	Manchester, Sheffield & Lincolnshire Railway.
MSJ&A	Manchester South Junction, & Altrincham Railway.
SA&M	Sheffield, Ashton-under-Lyne, & Manchester Railway.

First published 2017

Amberley Publishing
The Hill, Stroud,
Gloucestershire, GL5 4EP

www.amberley-books.com

Copyright © Anthony Dawson, 2017

The right of Anthony Dawson to be identified as the Author of this work has been asserted in accordance with the Copyrights, Designs and Patents Act 1988.

All rights reserved. No part of this book may be reprinted or reproduced or utilised in any form or by any electronic, mechanical or other means, now known or hereafter invented, including photocopying and recording, or in any information storage or retrieval system, without the permission in writing from the Publishers.

ISBN: 978 1 4456 6394 4 (print)
ISBN: 978 1 4456 6395 1 (ebook)

British Library Cataloguing in Publication Data.
A catalogue record for this book is available from the British Library.

Typeset in 10pt on 13pt Celeste.
Origination by Amberley Publishing.
Printed in the UK.

Contents

	Foreword	4
Chapter 1	Origins	5
Chapter 2	Building the Line	12
Chapter 3	Terminal Stations	46
Chapter 4	The Twentieth Century – Modernisation and Electrification	60
Chapter 5	Working the Woodhead	73
	Epilogue	90
	Select Bibliography	96

Foreword

As Chairman of the Woodhead Railway Heritage Group, it gives me great pleasure to write this new history of the Woodhead Railway. It is an iconic and scenic route, which has been adored by rail travellers, rail enthusiasts, and people out for afternoon car drives, who travel up to Woodhead to seek the glorious views to be had.

Many a story has been told since the line was built, opening in sections between 1941 and 1945, along with fond and happy memories; especially from those who worked along the Woodhead Railway.

As an avid rail enthusiast, I have my own happy memories of the busy days at Guide Bridge Station which all types of Freight trains that travelled over Woodhead, and the local commuter services travelling to Hadfield and back from Manchester Piccadilly which trundled through the station.

As a youngster I got to know quite a number of the staff based at Guide Bridge Station, where I spent many an hour either in the Station Masters office, Ashton Junction Signal Box, or sat in the Fuelling cabin brewing up for the drivers.

I was fortunate to have the opportunity to go out on a few trips with the drivers. One trip was on a summer Wednesday, when I rode in the brake van with Guard Ian Nicholson from Guide Bridge to the Woodhead Tunnel, when the track was being taken up. Once we got to the tunnel I made my way to the cab of the Class 47 locomotive as it pushed the wagons into the tunnel. Inside the tunnel the lights were still on, so I got a good view watching the track being lifted. Sadly I never had a camera to record the event, and some 30 years later, it is all but distant memories now.

Under the auspices of the Association of Community Rail Partnership Scheme, in 2015 I adopted my beloved Guide Bridge Station, where a team of volunteers have created an award winning Memorial Garden to remember those who once worked at Guide Bridge. The Woodhead Railway Heritage Group was founded in spring 2016. Our aim is not to reopen the Woodhead Railway, but to celebrate and protect what remains of the line. This book will share those memories that I had of the Woodhead Railway, and will bring back many fond memories for people who remember the Woodhead Railway as it was so many years ago.

Andy Kettle FdSc
Station Adopter Guide Bridge Station
Founder/Chairman Woodhead Railway Heritage Group

Chapter 1

Origins

The Sheffield & Manchester Railway

What was to become the Sheffield, Ashton-under-Lyne & Manchester Railway originates with the first railway boom of the 1830s. Less than a month after the opening of the Liverpool & Manchester Railway, the first committee meeting of the embryonic Sheffield & Manchester Railway was held in Sheffield on 4 November 1830, chaired by Nicholas Robinson Esq., a prosperous Liverpool corn merchant who served as mayor from 1828 to 1829. The railway to Sheffield was just one of seven schemes proposed during that month alone:

Bradford & Leeds
Liverpool & Leeds (competing with the Liverpool & Manchester)
Manchester & Huddersfield
Manchester & Leeds
Manchester & Sheffield
Oldham & Manchester
Sheffield & Goole

The engineer for this proposed line was George Stephenson, whose route – in order to avoid the main Pennine ridge – was via the Goyt Valley, Bugsworth, Chinley, Castleton and Hathersage. It would have involved numerous bridges and a good deal of tunnelling, at a cost of £600,000. As with the Liverpool & Manchester and later the Grand Junction railways, most of the capital came from Liverpool; Robert Gwynne of the National Railway Museum, York, has argued that money invested by Liverpool merchants in these early railway schemes was slavery compensation money. There was, however, doubt in the minds of many subscribers over the selected route: one correspondent to the *Sheffield Independent* believed the route was of too much importance to be 'left to one engineer', while another writing to the *Sheffield Courant* suggested an alternative route via Holmesfield, Calver, Middleton Dale and the Peak Forest, which would have been a more direct and easier undertaking. The *Sheffield Independent* was full of praise for the proposed railway, believing Sheffield to be, so miserably situated as regards the means of conveying its extensive and peculiar manufactures to other parts of the Kingdom, and to other countries of the world, we cannot but say that if there is advantage in, or necessary for, good, cheap, and rapid carriage of manufactures elsewhere, this advantage and this necessity will be felt pre-eminently here. (*Sheffield Independent*, 25 September 1830)

The Sheffield & Manchester Railway Act received Royal Assent on 23 August 1831; the capital was fixed at £530,000 with additional borrowing powers amounting to £176,000. The line was to connect with the L&M at Water Street in Manchester and run via Stockport, Marple, Whaley Bridge (terminus of the Cromford & High Peak Railway) and then to Sheffield. The *Sheffield Independent* heartily welcomed Parliamentary approval of the railway:

A large proportion of the manufacture of Sheffield is consumed in Lancashire or exported at Liverpool; and there is no other way to transport this merchandize than by horse and cart over the mountains of Derbyshire, which is very expensive, or by the circuitous route of ninety miles in length through the Yorkshire canals; and both lines of conveyance occasion an extraordinary sacrifice of time. (*Sheffield Independent*, 2 April 1831)

Furthermore, the railway would be a boon to Stockport because of the 'very defective' 'mode of transport' to that town, and that manufactured goods from Nottingham, Leicester and Derby could be quickly and easily shipped to Manchester and thence the docks at Liverpool, or via the proposed Sheffield & Goole Railway to Hull.

Obtaining their Act had cost the company £11,939 14s 11d out of a subscribed £21,631 15s 3d. A further £2,775 10s 3d had been spent on the application for the 'Stockport Junction Railway'. The first Stockport Junction Railway Bill had been read in May 1830; it was fiercely opposed by 'Mr Egerton of Tatton [Park]', which was the 'principal cause of the Bill being lost'. By November 1830, however, Egerton had decided to withdraw all opposition to the Stockport line and, along with 'all the other principal landowners', opposition to the Sheffield & Manchester Railway as a whole. A second Stockport Junction Railway, also engineered by George Stephenson, was proposed in 1834, commencing in Stockport 'on the Lancashire side of the river, near the Wellington Bridge, proceeded in a direct line to the railway at Warrington, branches off near Didsbury to Manchester, on one side, and on the other ... probably to the canal at Poynton.'

The company was left with a mere £7,500 with which to build their railway. The route surveyed by Stephenson was modified to make it more practicable to locomotives by abandoning 'the most objectionable part of the inclined planes, at Rushop Edge' by diverting the line through Edale, reducing the summit by 300 feet and the ruling gradient to 1:36. The inclined planes were to be worked by stationary engines and the predicted heavy limestone traffic from Derbyshire was to be gravity worked, reducing the number of locomotives needed to a bare minimum. In order to attract passenger traffic, the company would reduce the cost of second class and parcels 'to one half the present coach fare', but much worry was occasioned by passengers having to travel through several lengthy tunnels. The *Sheffield Independent*, however, struck a gloomy chord by reminding its readers of 'the extreme depression in the money market at this time,' which would make it difficult for the company to borrow additional capital. Furthermore, the directors voted 'not to proceed with every part of the line' but to build it and operate it in stages. There obviously appears to have been difficulty in garnering support for the scheme; in December 1831 and again in March 1832 'at a Discount, a large number of shares' were advertised for sale in Sheffield and Liverpool.

A general meeting of the company and subscribers was held at the York Hotel, Manchester, on 11 April 1832, chaired by Nicholas Robinson, 'to inquire into the prospects and practicability of the undertaking'. It was proposed to either repeal the 'objectionable Clauses in the present Act,' to survey an easier route or to abandon the entire scheme. The company struggled on for a further year: the directors resolved to 'give up the undertaking' at a special meeting held in Manchester on 20 June 1833.

The Sheffield, Ashton-under-Lyne and Manchester Railway

Despite the failure of the Sheffield & Manchester, the demand for a railway from Sheffield to Manchester was still high; the first meeting of a provisional committee of fifty-six 'influential gentlemen' was held to promote a new railway scheme between the two towns on 4 January 1836 in the Cutler's Hall, Sheffield, chaired by Lord Wharncliffe. There was a second meeting in Manchester on the following day. Wharncliffe, born Mr Stuart-Wortley but elevated to the Peerage in 1826, was MP for Yorkshire (from 1818) and one of the 'Grand Allies' of coal owners in the North East, together with Lord Ravensworth and the Earl of Strathmore. He was a keen proponent of the railways; despite having presided over the Parliamentary Committee, which rejected Robert Stephenson's London & Birmingham Railway, he was one of sixteen peers and thirty-three MPs who supported the railway and oversaw its passage through Parliament. Sadly, he would die days before the Woodhead Route was completed. Charles Blacker Vignoles was appointed as engineer; he had

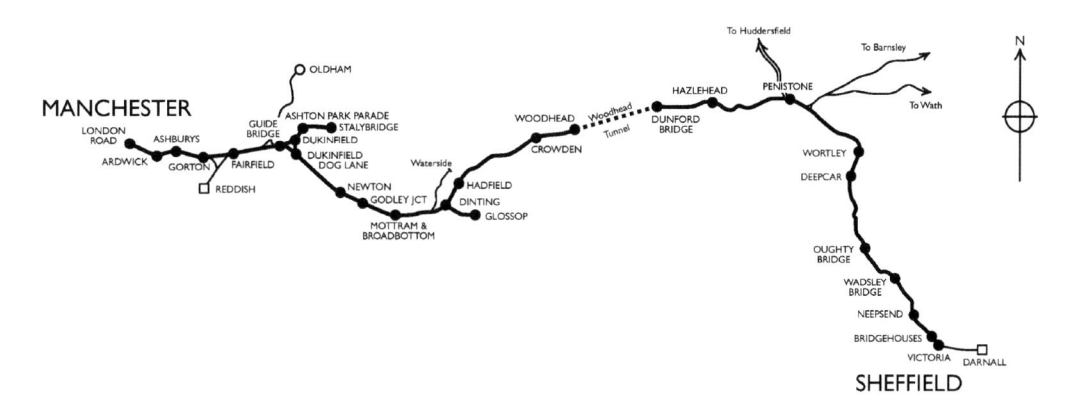

Map of the Woodhead Route – the Manchester and Sheffield main line is shown in bold. (Andy Mason)

7

completed his survey and started marking out the route in 1835, but its completion had been delayed by the 'inclemency of the season'. He reported:

> The connexion between Sheffield, Manchester, and Liverpool has so long been desired, that I have no occasion to argue its expediency ... the high price of carriage [of goods] may be lowered by one third, and one half ... Independent of the immediate connexion between Sheffield and Manchester, the route proposed will pass by the coalfields quarries and minerals of the valley of the River Dun [sic Don], and through a populous and flourishing district of Lancashire, filled with factories. Short branches will afford access to the important towns of Glossop, Ashton, Staley Bridge, and the adjacent manufacturing districts and villages. (*Sheffield Independent,* 9 January 1836)

Furthermore, Vignoles told the committee that

> I cannot forebear urging the importance, to the town of Sheffield, to avail itself of an opportunity of obtaining a direct railway communication, from Sheffield, with the main lines of railway to the metropolis, by Chesterfield; which ... will bring a further supply of excellent coal from the valley of the Rother.

Lord Wharncliffe (1776–1845). Born Mr James Stuart-Wortley, and created 1st Baron Wharncliffe in 1826, he was an influential supporter of early railway schemes.

Charles Blacker Vignoles (1796–1875), first engineer to the Sheffield, Ashton-under-Lyne & Manchester Railway before his fall from grace in 1839.

This junction with the North Midland Railway would have proceeded via Attercliffe, Darnal and the Rother Valley to Chesterfield. Vignoles also proposed a junction with the Liverpool & Manchester as well as a station at Store Street, to be shared with the 'proposed Cheshire Junction Railway' (i.e., the Manchester & Birmingham). The station in Sheffield was to be approached by a mile-long 'lofty viaduct'. Representatives from Manchester not only supported junctions with other lines entering the city but also a far-sighted joint terminal station that would have changed railway history in Manchester considerably:

> There were three lines which might affect the present, – The Manchester and Leeds, the Stockport and Manchester, and the line from Store-street, Manchester, to join in Cheshire the line from Birmingham to Newton ... It was desirable ... to see whether the various projects might not introduce some new features, as to a Terminus in Manchester ... It would be desirable for the Manchester and Liverpool to join with the others ... if they were to join the Leeds and Manchester, it would be an advantage ... And if several companies were to unite in making the terminus it would simplify the matter considerably and relieve them of much expense in the approach to Manchester.

Considerable doubt was expressed as to the ruling gradients of the chosen route; Vignoles suggested that 'an inclination of forty feet in one mile' was practicable and workable by locomotives, citing the Stockton & Darlington, the Leeds & Selby and even one American example. He also thought that the ruling gradient was in favour of carrying goods to Sheffield ('the whole of the traffic to Sheffield will be descending') and that time lost in ascending the line to the summit could be regained on the descent. The *Bradford Observer* (14 January 1836) remarked that locomotives of 25 hp could draw a load of 100 tons 'up the inclined plane at a rate of six miles an hour ... and thirty on the descent'. The journey time would be two-and-a-half hours with a 'heavy load' and two hours with a light one.

A prospectus was issued in May 1836; the total cost of the scheme was estimated by Vignoles to be £800,000, which would rise to £1 million by 1838. The line was to proceed from Manchester via Ashton-Under-Lyne, Glossop and Woodhead (where there was a

2-mile tunnel) and Penistone to Sheffield. There was a short branch to Stalybridge. The prospectus stated that

> The present mode of conveyance of goods to and from Sheffield and Manchester is by waggon, and the time occupied in transit is about forty hours; there is not the remote possibility of any competition by water, and consequently the exclusive carriage of merchandise and minerals between the two termini which can be taken by the railway at two thirds of the present cost and in one tenth the time, may be calculated upon as a prolific and unfailing source of revenue. The intermediate districts including Glossop, Hyde, Mottram, Newton, Dukinfield, Ashton Under Lyne and Staley-Bridge will be, by this railway, so united to Manchester, as to derive all the advantages of conducting the trade of the extensive and important place and at the same time retain those peculiar to their several localities. In addition to these important benefits, inexhaustible supplies of coal, of the best quality, and of paviours, slate, ashlar and other stone, abounding upon the line and for which there is immense and increasing demand will be opened.

The Provisional Committee asked for a second opinion from Joseph Locke, one-time apprentice to George Stephenson, who was winning fame building the Grand Junction Railway. He and Vignoles presented their surveys to the committee on 14 October 1836; the differences between the two surveys having been reconciled, the final proposals were tabled on 25 November 1836. In order to constrain the ruling gradients to 1:100, the length of the tunnel at Woodhead was increased from 2 to 3 miles; the branch to Stalybridge was to be extended by moving the proposed junction to Guide Bridge from Ashton-Under-Lyne, which would now be bypassed. So too was Glossop. Vignoles estimated that passenger trains could travel between the two towns in two-and-a-half hours, and that freight (up to 60 tons) would take no more than four hours. He also assured the public that it would take no more than ten minutes to traverse the Woodhead Tunnel – then the longest in the country – and that lamps would be provided for all the passenger coaches. Locke went on to add that in 'no distant period' the Manchester–Sheffield route would become a through route between the East and West Coasts. The Bill to incorporate the Sheffield, Ashton-Under-Lyne & Manchester Railway was deposited at the end of November and passed through Parliament with little opposition, receiving Royal Assent on 5 May 1837.

The first general meeting of the company was held in Sheffield at the Cutler's Hall on 23 October 1837 at 1 p.m., chaired by Lord Wharncliffe, to 'proceed in the Execution of an Act of Parliament' to build the railway. The railway was to be built and then operated in stages as each section was completed. The directors, however, were rapidly losing heart: they had advertised a capital of £1 million in £100 shares, but shareholders were slow in coming forward. There was considerable doubt about whether the railway could be built at all, with a flurry of correspondence in the Manchester, Sheffield and London newspapers discussing the relative merits of the scheme and whether it could ever be made to pay. According to his biographer, Vignoles had to reassure the directors to sway their mistrust, 'which naturally arose in the minds of persons unfamiliar with Public Works on a large Scale, who having no standard of comparison in their own minds whereto to refer the projected measures, will often condemn them as impracticable'. The directors advised Vignoles to build the line with 'all due economy' but the situation was becoming critical:

a shareholders' meeting in Sheffield that autumn proposed to stop all work on the line and to postpone calls on shares until the following year. Under the law, until all shares had been subscribed, the company could not invoke its compulsory powers; eventually the Act would become null and void. Vignoles had already purchased 100 shares in the company – under the name of Miss Hutton – and now started buying up a large quantity (ultimately 1,402) of the depreciated shares, hoping to assuage the sense of unease among the shareholders and directors alike – as well as make himself a pretty profit at the end of it all. This scheme, however, would later end in disaster for Vignoles.

The fortunes of the company began to recover in spring 1838 and, by March, the company had once again decided to recommence work. A second prospectus was issued in June 1838. At a special meeting of the directors in Sheffield on 24 September 1838 it was announced that the first contract to build the railway had been let to Messrs Smith, Eckersby & Worswick. The line was to join with the Manchester & Birmingham Railway at

> Chancery-Lane, Ardwick, thence by the Pottery at Gorton to within 900 yards of Ashton-under-Lyne. Proceeding in a direct line, it passes over the River Tame and Peak Forest Canal, at Duckinford [*sic* Dukinfield], to the Dewsnup colliery close by the village of Newton-Green, crossing the new turnpike road from Hyde to Mottram, through Godley and Hattersley, to the river Etherow or Mersey at Broadbottom; it then goes near the reservoirs of Mr Potter's print works, within half-a-mile of Glossop, by Dinting Dale, to the entrance of the tunnel by Saltersbrook: after passing through the tunnel the line will by the valley of the Don, by Peniston, Ospring and Wortley, to the terminus in Sheffield. (*Morning Post*, 12 October 1838)

The Cutler's Hall, Sheffield: home of the Company of Cutlers in Hallamshire, built in 1832 by Samuel Bromhead Taylor. The dignity of Master Cutler was established in 1624.

Chapter 2

Building the Line

The first sod was ceremonially cut by the chairman, Lord Wharncliffe, on 1 October 1838, on the site of the western entrance of the Woodhead Tunnel. At 1.45 p.m., Lord Wharncliffe, accompanied by two of his sons, arrived by carriage from Wortley Hall. Accompanied by Vignoles, Lord Wharncliffe 'cut and drew out a sod and declared the ground duly broken'; Vignoles cut the next sod, followed by each of the directors in turn. Following this ceremony 'the company adjourned to an excellent collation in the principal marquee.' 'The repast being over', Lord Wharncliffe rose and spoke:

> This is one of the greatest communications (for the Leeds and Manchester line must also be taken into account) between the two largest, and most flourishing counties in the north; and I flatter myself that this railway will open out advantages to the towns of Sheffield and Manchester such as are little experienced at present.

By spring 1839 the entire line had been staked out, and tenders were advertised nationally in May and June 1839. Work commenced on the first – Ardwick – section soon after.

Viaducts and Bridges

Progress was initially rapid; the *Manchester Times* (23 October 1841) reports that the five-arch viaduct over the Tame at Dukinfield had been completed by that date:

> A handsome brick erection of five arches, each of considerable span, crossing the river Tame and exhibits the appearance of a firm, substantial piece of masonry.

The nine-arch Godley Viaduct was also complete, but of all the major engineering works so far completed, the *Manchester Times* sang the praises of stone and timber Etherow Viaduct, constructed by the contractor Richard Hattersley:

Alfred Jee's magnificent millstone grit and timber viaduct crossing the Etherow at Broadbottom in 1842: it was 42 metres high and 155 metres long.

> An erection of lofty and beautiful arches, with stone piers, crossing the river Mersey. The centre arch is of 150 feet span, and the other two of 120 feet each. (*Sheffield Iris*, 18 February 1843)

The *Illustrated London News* waxed lyrical about the viaduct:

> Never, perhaps, since the great Telford stretched the arm of his powerful genius across the Menai Straits ... has the world of science seen a work more worthy of regard than the one now under notice, for its boldness, grandeur and simplicity; showing as it does perfect command over the resources at hand and beautiful economy in their disposal ... Mr Locke whose name stands deservedly high ... may with truth be satisfied with this bold effort of his genius. Its strength and beauty are at once apparent; whilst the cheapness of its construction forms one, and not the least, of its recommendations as a study for imitation.

The viaduct was made from laminated timber, braced together with iron tie-rods and timber cross members supported on two massive millstone grit columns, rising to a height of 136 feet. The total cost was around £25,000; it had taken fifteen months to build.

The Dinting Viaduct was more spectacular still, consisting of five laminated timber main arches of 130 feet span, approached by eleven masonry arches of 50 feet span. It was 1,455 feet long and soared to a height of 125 feet. Construction started in 1842 and

Jee's viaduct over 170 years later.

was completed by August 1844 when it was inspected by General Pasley, HM Inspector of Railways. The *Sheffield Independent* believed the Dinting Viaduct to be

> One of the finest Railway Works in the Kingdom, and reflects the highest credit upon the company's Engineer, who designed it, Mr Alfred Jee, and Messrs. Buxton and Clarke the contractors, who have completed it in so satisfactory manner ... The picturesque scenery in the neighbourhood renders the effect of this Viaduct, crossing the valley at so great an elevation very striking, and calls forth the admiration of all beholders. (*Sheffield Independent* 10 August 1844)

A special train, driven by Jee himself and containing the directors and invited guests, was run over the viaduct; it left Glossop and crossed the viaduct 'amidst the cheers of the workmen' who had laboured on it.

Among supporters of the railway coming to Glossop was Edmund Potter, of Dinting Lodge, a wealthy Unitarian calico printer who had established his printing works at Dinting Vale in 1837; thanks to the arrival of the railway, Glossop became 'a regional centre of trade'. By 1862 Edmund Potter & Son was the largest calico printer in the world. Edmund's granddaughter was the novelist and naturalist Beatrix Potter.

Despite this praise, twelve years later the civil engineer recommended that some £350 be set aside per annum for the reconstruction of the Etherow Viaduct and £500 for that at Dinting Dale (*Sheffield Independent*, 3 February 1855).

An early colour postcard of the Dinting Arches: 38 metres high and 443 metres long.

The Dinting Arches still standing tall, 172 years after they were built: a lasting tribute to the ambition of the Sheffield, Ashton-under-Lyne & Manchester Railway.

Glossop station in British Railways days, 31 May 1964: the stone lion marks the private entrance of the Duke of Norfolk, at whose expense the Glossop branch was built.

The same scene over fifty years later: most of the station building has been put over to commercial use and only a single platform face remains in use. The line has also been singled.

16

Now above a pharmacy, the Duke's lion still stands guard over Glossop station. (Author)

The timber viaducts lasted for about twenty years; in October 1859 it was decided to strengthen them and Sir William Fairbairn of Manchester was consulted about replacing both with an iron structure. Tubular or box-girder bridges were built in 1860 on the existing piers. By 1893, however, it was found to be necessary to strengthen both of these bridges with additional girders, and in 1919 three extra piers were built at Etherow and nine at Dinting to support the viaducts.

It was on the Dinting Viaduct in September 1855 that three passengers – John Healey, Jane Hadfield (reportedly the lover of Healey) and Thomas Priestnall – lost their lives: a Manchester & Sheffield train was stopped on the viaduct at 9.35 p.m. to allow a 'Liverpool excursion train' to 'discharge passengers at the station [Hadfield].' Sadly, however,

> The night was very dark, and it appears some of the passengers in the Manchester train, who had to get out at Hadfield, imagined that this train was already at the station. Three of these persons, two young men and a young woman, succeeded in opening the door of the carriages and got out. The parapet of the viaduct on that side was within a very short space of the carriages, and it is supposed owing to the darkness of the night, instead of getting down in the narrow space between the train and the parapet of the viaduct, they stepped out upon the top of the parapet. Immediately afterwards an alarm was given that they had fallen over, and the shocking fact was afterwards confirmed ... they had fallen a height of seventy-five feet. (*Reynolds's Newspaper*, 23 September 1855)

Following the inquest, it was recommended that trains were to no longer stop on the viaduct, to 'remove the signal station so much nearer Manchester' and install 'a rail or some sufficient fence ... to prevent recurrence of similar accidents.'

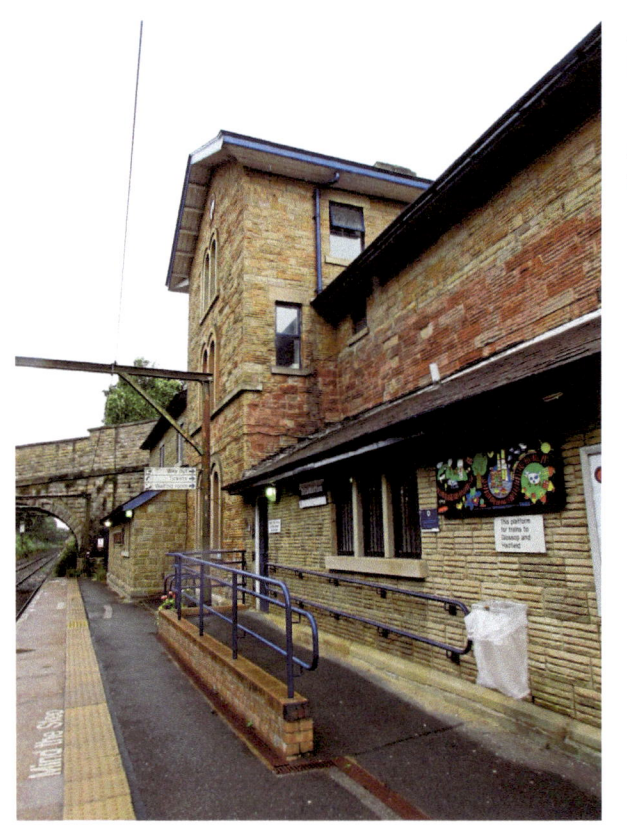

Above: Broadbottom station, photographed from the train on 5 May 1963.

Left: The same view, fifty-three years later.

18

The elegant skew bridge at the end of Broadbottom station.

Looking like a giant Nonconformist Chapel, Broadbottom goods shed today houses the Etherow Centre for outdoor pursuits.

Two years later there was a serious accident on the Etherow Viaduct, involving the 10.55 a.m. Manchester–London train operated by the Sheffield & Great Northern Railway on Tuesday 3 November 1857. The short train, consisting of six carriages 'carrying from a dozen to twenty passengers', derailed while crossing the viaduct at speed. One passenger recalled that

> When close upon the viaduct, the train proceeding at express speed, the carriages got off the line, and the sudden jerk detached them from the engine which dashed on faster than ever without them. The carriages were thrown off on the outer side of the rails, and, in coming in violent contact with a wall ... were completely shattered, their sides literally being torn away. (*Liverpool Mercury,* 4 November 1857)

The *Manchester Guardian* continued in more measured tones:

> The train ... ran off the rails when approaching a very high viaduct over the river Etherow ... but most providently did not leave the line, though the sides of the carriage came into contact with the battlement of the viaduct, by which they were very considerably damaged. There were only six passengers on the train, none of whom were hurt, though all were most seriously alarmed, as the viaduct is so high, that if the train had gone over it is difficult to conceive how anybody in it would have survived.

The accident was due to what we would now term a 'signalling error'. Track on the viaduct was undergoing 'repairs and renewals' and 'the signalman, who, as usual, was stationed 800 yards from the spot ... neglected to give the proper caution' so that

> The driver of the train went over the incomplete portion of the road, at an average of 30 miles an hour instead of half speed. Of the six carriages ... four were thrown off the line, but, strange to say, the engine and tender kept to the track. Two of the carriages struck against the end pier of the viaduct, one having its end and the other its side smashed by the violence of the concussion. (*Ashton Weekly Reporter,* 7 November 1857)

At this point the couplings snapped and 'two first and one second class carriages ran forward, grazing along the wooden parapet for about fifty yards' when 'the foremost of these carriages struck another pier, the engine and the first van broke loose, and after proceeding another hundred yards or so, came to a stand.'

The Dinting Viaduct was the scene of a collision in February 1865 when two goods trains collided early in the morning: 'the enginemen and firemen of both trains had a very narrow escape' and 'fortunately there was no loss of life.' The collision, however, was so severe as to block the line causing considerable delay throughout the day. Eleven years later, fireman Stevens of the Great Northern Railway, one half of the footplate crew of the 10 a.m. 'Up' from Liverpool and Manchester to London, 'fell off the engine while the train was running at great speed over the Dinting Viaduct and sustained terrible injuries.'

On February 6 1884 a train de-railed crossing the viaduct when 'an axle of one of the carriages broke just as the train was passing over Dinting Viaduct ... The carriage, which contained five people, was dragged along the viaduct and finally struck the Dinting Station

The unusual triangular station at Dinting; the former MS&L/Great Central platforms on 20 April 1964.

The surviving buildings at Dinting, 2016.

21

The mechanical signal box at Dinting, slated for closure in 2019.

platform.' Happily no one was hurt, but the line was blocked until 5 a.m. the following day. Four years later in September 1888 another train derailed on the viaduct: 'the engine left the rails and went over the sleepers for about twenty yards dragging the coaches with it.' Rails were 'displaced and sleepers displaced' but no one was hurt. The line was blocked for 'six or seven hours'.

The Woodhead Tunnel

Work on the first of the iconic Woodhead tunnels was commenced by Vignoles in February 1837 when he proposed sinking the first of eleven shafts (or 'eyes') equidistantly along the course of the tunnel; work that he estimated would take at least twelve months. From these 'eyes' a driftway would be dug to connect each of them to 'prove the practicability of driving [the] tunnels'. A year later it was proposed to reduce the tunnel in scale to one single-track bore. This new tunnel would have been in a class of its own: 3 miles long (5,000 yards), driven through solid millstone grit. Robert Stephenson's Kilsby Tunnel was a mere 2,420 yards and Brunel's famous Box Tunnel 3,230 yards. On 19 April 1839 Vignoles presented a revised plan for the Woodhead Tunnel, which, after much discussion, was formally adopted by the directors in June. The tunnel was to be of twin single-track bores, each 12 feet wide and 18 feet high, measuring 16 feet from centre to centre and leaving a solid wall of stone 20 feet wide between each tunnel. The southern tunnel would be constructed first; fourteen exploratory shafts were to be sunk along the centre line between the two tunnels, followed by six 'eyes' 9 feet in diameter. From these 'drifts' 4 feet 6 inches wide and 5 feet high would be dug, from which the main tunnel would be opened after the drifts had been connected along the entire length of the tunnel. The tunnel was to be 3 miles 13 yards long, rising from 857 feet above sea level at Woodhead on a gradient of 1:200 to the summit at Dunford Bridge at 943 feet.

Tenders were placed for construction of the tunnel as well as adverts for

> Miners. Wanted: A Quantity of Miners at the WOODHEAD TUNNEL on the Sheffield, Ashton-under-Lyne and Manchester Railway. Good workmen will meet with employment and liberal Wages by applying to Mr Richard Hattersley, the Contractor.

Vignoles also demonstrated a new 'boring machine':

> It is sent to him by his son in Germany. It is worked by ropes, and capable of penetrating a twelve inch bore, at six feet per day, through a solid rock. The importance of such an effective and ingenious instrument in a work like the Sheffield and Manchester Railway need not be expatiated upon.

In March 1839 Vignoles was able to report to the directors the results of the trial shafts and drifts:

Woodhead station (built 1861) and the western portals of the Tunnel, c. 1900.

The eastern portals at Dunford Bridge, c. 1900.

> In a few weeks I will submit the Models, Drawings and Details of the Tunnel, the operations for opening up the western face. The result of the boring, as far as it has gone, and further careful examination of the dip in the strata, and of the bassetings along, and in the vicinity of the line, fully confirm my original conception, and satisfy me that the material in the Tunnel will be hard throughout, and that the whole may be economically worked. The time is now-arrived when the drill-way from the western end, and the working shafts, should be forthwith commenced, and the boring be resumed, as soon as accommodation can be found for the workmen, by the erection of cottages, shops & c., a want of which, has severely retarded during the late severe weather, the works above Woodhead. (*Sheffield Independent*, 2 March 1839)

The *Sheffield Independent* (4 May 1839) reported that the works on the tunnel were progressing 'very favourably' and in August Vignoles reported that the contract for the western end and portal of the Tunnel had been let to Messrs. Smith, Eckersley and Woswick, but apparently on terms that were 'not advantageous' to the company. He also reported that the 'Tunnels, the Shafts, Driftways and Engines have been contracted for with *respectable parties*' and he felt able to inform the directors that the railway would be constructed 'nearly to the Parliamentary Estimate'. A special 'Tunnel Sub-Committee' was appointed to oversee the works on the Woodhead Tunnel and a new engineer, William Cooper, was appointed to direct the work. In June 1839 it was reported that the western face driftways had penetrated 63 yards and the eastern 52 yards. The five 'eyes' had reached a depth of 20 yards but work was halted, as the existing pumping engines could not cope with water ingress.

Vignoles, however, was chafing under the terms of his agreement with the directors; indeed his relationship with them had always been difficult. His contract as Engineer-in-Chief was due to expire in 1839 but he had little doubt that he would be re-appointed. Far more serious was the matter of the 1,402 shares he had purchased on the cheap two years earlier. So far no calls had been made on them but, in summer 1839, the directors, needing additional capital to push on their railway, called them in: Vignoles was faced with a sudden demand for over £14,000. At a meeting on 24 October 1839, Lord Wharncliffe drew attention to the difficulties with regards to Vignoles's shares and, after a long discussion, the Board decided that Vignoles should forfeit his entire stock of shares in the company. Vignoles therefore resigned in December and was succeeded by Joseph Locke as Engineer-in-Chief, who was ably assisted by Alfred Jee as his resident engineer.

By August 1842 driftways three, four and five had been commenced and some 3,032 yards of the tunnel had been excavated; driftways one and two were expected to be started by September of that year. A major problem with the tunnelling operations was keeping the water out and, after the installation of new pumping engines, Alfred Jee was able to report that the navvies were making 80 yards headway per week. The tunnel was driven through solid millstone grit, tunnelling from each end toward the centre and via the five vertical shafts. In each shaft was a 20-hp steam engine working a pump to drain the working levels. Some 157 tons of gunpowder were used in the blasting.

The living and working conditions for the navvies were appalling; work on the tunnel went on for twenty-fours hours, seven days a week, with the men working in twelve-hour shifts:

> Hundreds of men ... whose huts form a scattered encampment extending three and four miles in length over the bleak, hilly moor ... The huts are a curiosity. They are mostly of stone without mortar, the roof of thatch or flags, erected by the men for their own temporary use ... many of the huts were filthy dens ...

As many as fifteen men lived crammed together in each of these huts. They were poorly paid and had to pay extortionate prices for food and drink in the 'Tommy Shops'. Drunkenness and violence – particularly between the English and Irish workers – was commonplace. Some twenty-six men died during the construction of the tunnel, but finally it was opened at a cost of £200,000 on 22 December 1845. The working and living conditions of the navvies led to national outrage. Social reformer Edwin Chadwick and the Manchester Statistical Society published three papers damning the treatment of the navvies: 'Thirty-two killed ... and one hundred and forty wounded, besides the sick ... losses in this one work may be stated as more than 3 per cent killed, and 14 per cent wounded.' He dramatically concluded that this rate of mortality was higher than many battles of the Peninsular War. The radical, Unitarian-owned and -edited *Manchester Guardian* drew attention to the plight of the navvies, but the contractor, John Nicholson, published his own paper to defend his own working practices, stating that most of the accidents were due to negligence, and certainly not to drunkenness as Chadwick *et al* had suggested. The Woodhead controversy resulted in a Parliamentary Select Committee on Railway Labourers. The finished tunnel was on a rising gradient of 1:201 from west to east; the arch was in the form of a semi-ellipse, with a maximum width of 15 feet and 18 feet high. There were two open drainage gullies running in the cess. Controversies aside, the *Sheffield Iris* thought the tunnel 'a wondrous triumph of art over nature':

A double-headed Sheffield-bound express plunges into the darkness of Woodhead 2 as it crosses a Manchester express exiting Woodhead 1.

> [it] may be pronounced the greatest engineering work of the kind which has yet been consummated. So accurately was it driven from the faces under the calculations of the Engineer, that the bores met within a few inches and so direct is the line of perforation that when standing at the eastern entrance we had no difficulty in observing daylight at the other end appearing like a small burning taper or candle light in a dark cupboard ...

The tunnel was single line, and so to ensure against accidents Cooke & Wheatstone's 'patent magnetic telegraph' was installed at Woodhead and Dunford Bridge stations in order to despatch and receive trains through the tunnel. Furthermore, a pilot engine fitted with an extra-bright 'argand lamp with a large polished metal disc for reflection, so that a powerful beam of light was thrown forward' was stationed at the tunnel and attached to every train that passed through. Despite these precautions, accidents still happened; in October 1847 the 1.30 p.m. goods train from Sheffield came to grief in the tunnel when

> A quantity of railway bars [rails] with which the first wagon was laden, fell onto the line. The consequence was, that nearly every waggon (the train containing 30 trucks), was thrown off the line, and jammed up in dreadful confusion in that dark and gloomy situation. On the first jerk being given to the engine, the stoker was fortunate enough to succeed in unhooking the coupling chain that attached the tender to the first carriage, and the driver putting on more steam at that moment, the engine and tender shot away out of danger ... the obstruction was of course complete. (*Derbyshire Mercury*, 3 November 1847)

The accident disrupted traffic for the entire day. The *Derbyshire Mercury* reported that passengers had to walk 'a distance of four miles' between Woodhead and Dunford Bridge stations. The line appears to have always been vulnerable to the weather; in July 1846 the line was blocked by a landslip caused by heavy rain at the Woodhead end. Traffic was suspended and 150 workmen were needed to clear the line. In August 1849 a freak summer storm ('without a parallel for the last fourteen or fifteen years') flooded Dunford Bridge station and blocked the line. In December 1876 the traffic through the tunnel was suspended, due to heavy winter rain causing the central wall of the tunnel in the Down tunnel at the Sheffield end to 'bulge out considerably'. Traffic was suspended and, while the wall was being stabilised, single-line working was adopted.

Having only a single-track tunnel, however, soon proved to be a bottleneck. One of the first acts of the new Board of the MS&L was proposed at a meeting held at Normanton on 30 September 1846. Work on the second bore was begun in the following year but cholera broke out among the workers and very quickly claimed twenty-eight lives. The second bore opened on 2 February 1852. A new, larger station was opened at Woodhead in 1861. There was a series of accidents at Woodhead in the winter of 1874/75. The first was in November when

> A portion of the goods train became accidentally detached ... and ran down the incline ... till stopped by collision with another goods train, which was also coming to Penistone on the same line of rails. In the collision, the guard of the runaway train, William Henry Williamson, was injured, and a platelayer, James Davis, who leaped on the [brake] van at Woodhead to assist in putting on the brake, was also injured ... In the collision several wagons were damaged, and the line was blocked so as to delay trains from the south for an hour and a half to two hours. (*Sheffield & Rotherham Independent,* 19 November 1874)

In March 1875 a goods train collided with a 'platelayer's trolley [which] had been, by some unexplained means, left on the line' in the Woodhead Tunnel. The trolley was 'smashed to pieces' and much damage was done to the permanent way and to 'several of the goods wagons'. The line was 'in consequence blocked for some hours, but the tunnel being a double one the other set of metals were not affected'. There was, however, a 'great accumulation of traffic until arrangements were made for working on the single line system.'

Just over a year later, a Great Northern express from Manchester to King's Cross collided with local goods train from Sheffield to Manchester at Woodhead due to a signalling error. Another serious collision occurred two years later when another Great Northern train collided with a goods train. At 6.30 a.m., a fish train from Lincoln to Manchester was checked by signals when 'the London and Liverpool (Great Northern) express goods... ran violently into it':

> The break van and four wagons belonging to the Lincoln train were completely smashed and scattered, while the engine and three wagons of the Liverpool [GNR] train were completely done for – at least if the engine be not irretrievably crippled, it is very badly broken indeed. Some eight or nine other wagons left the line. (*Sheffield & Rotherham Independent,* 28 October 1876)

Fortunately no one was killed or injured but a 'great deal of damage was done' to the platform and the permanent way, blocking the line for several hours. The contemporary press reported that the line was 'worked on the block system, and the Liverpool train should have been detained at Woodhead until the Lincoln train (stopped at Crowden) had cleared

Left: The row of now-derelict railway cottages overlooking Crowden station.

Below: The site of Crowden station, summer 2016.

The western portals of the Woodhead Tunnels, summer 2016.

The Dunford Bridge portal of Woodhead 3, summer 2016.

the next block section.' The signalmen at Woodhead and Crowden were both suspended because of their negligence. There was a repeat performance of the same accident in New Year 1878, when another GNR express goods train 'ran at full speed into a stationary goods train' and 'smashed up most of the latter' at Woodhead.

During 1882 Edward Watkin proposed widening the tunnel to enable the track to be quadrupled through it. It was estimated that the cost would be £200,000 with a further £50,000 for a 'nine-foot drift' from end to end of the tunnel to improve its drainage. Watkin also proposed the use of electric lighting in the tunnel rather than kerosene lamps.

Opening the Line

The first section of the line was opened 17 November 1841, from Ardwick Junction to 'the viaduct over the turnpike road at Godley toll-bar, a distance of eight to nine miles.' The *Sheffield Independent* of 30 October 1841 noted that 'all is wanting to complete this portion of the railway is a short portion of the embankment necessary to form a junction with the Manchester and Birmingham line, at Chancery Lane.' The same newspaper opined that

> The portion of the Manchester and Sheffield Railway about to be opened traverses a district studded with populous manufacturing towns and villages; and amongst them we may mention, as the most important, Gorton, Openshaw, Audenshaw, Hooley Hill, Fairfield, Ashton-under-Lyne, Stalybridge, Dukinfield, Tintwistle, Hollinwood, Newton, and Hyde.

The line ran on 'a considerable embankment' out of Manchester 'for a mile and three-quarters' before plunging into a cutting at Openshaw, where it passed under the Stockport Canal and under Lee Street. From there it 'passes with few exceptions ... as embankments, through cuttings or on the surface of the ground ... so that it may be presumed there is little likelihood of any interruption after it is once opened from slippings, settlings or other accidents to which embankments are liable.' The first station reached was Fairfield, for Gorton.

Next was Guide Bridge:

> The station for the accommodation of Ashton is established at Guide Bridge, about three-quarters of a mile from the new Church; and this station will also accommodate the traffic with Hooley Hill station, at Dog Lane, near Dukinfield Hall. The line passes through the township and traverses the extensive coal fields of Messrs. Swire and Lees, and of the Dukinfield Coal Company. The station here will be the point also at which the traffic of Stalybridge and neighbourhood must come upon the line. The next station is Newton Green, established for the convenience of the populous townships of Newton and Hyde. The next station is at Godley, on the Mottram and Hyde turnpike road, for the present terminus of the line. (*Sheffield Independent*, 30 October 1841)

A station at Gorton was opened in 1842 in a 'temporary wooden hut' placed at the 'Green Lane [level] Crossing'. This was replaced in July 1848 following the diversion of Green Lane,

Fairfield (for Gorton) in steam days: one of the few stations in the Manchester area to have six platform faces.

Fairfield over a century later, reduced to only two platform faces.

31

Guide Bridge station, c. 1930s, when it was a major junction with routes to Oldham via Ashton, Stalybridge and onwards to Sheffield.

The surviving buildings on the north side (Platform 1) at Guide Bridge; the track at Platform 2 was lifted in 1989 and the buildings demolished. Those on Platform 1 are going to be home to the new Woodhead Railway Heritage Centre.

and the opening of an iron-girder bridge carrying the lane over the railway. Onwards traffic for Hollinwood, Tintwistle and Glossop were to be handled at Godley and arrangements 'had been made by which the Sheffield coaches and carriers will meet the trains there, for the accommodation of "through" traffic.' The line was built as a single track, with no passing places and operated on the basis of 'one engine in steam' – a train left Manchester for Godley and no train was allowed to depart Godley until the Manchester train had arrived.

A further bottleneck was that both the SA&M and M&B trains used the same single line in and out of London Road. The *Manchester Guardian* opined

> Some caution will be requisite here to prevent two trains ... coming into contact at this point. This, of course, may be done by arranging the times, or keeping the rails separate ... at present the proper precaution seems to be to stand a watchman there to keep a look-out on both lines, and see that when a train is arriving on one line, there is no train arriving on the other, or if there be, to make the signal to one of them to slacken speed. (*Manchester Guardian,* 20 November 1841)

Very rapidly single-track working was found to be inconvenient and a passing loop was installed at Ashton & Hooley Hill, and the line was doubled as far as Newton in 1842. The second section to be opened was that from Godley to Broadbottom on 10 December 1842 and a fortnight later, on Christmas Eve, the line was open through to Glossop, as Dinting was then referred to, before the opening of the branch through to Glossop (9 June 1845).

Gorton station in LNER days, 1930s, when it had four platform faces.

The same scene today, revealing Gorton in reduced circumstances, with only two platform faces.

The third section, from Dinting to Woodhead via Hadfield, was opened on 8 August 1844, following its inspection by General Pasley the day before. The *Sheffield Independent* (10 August 1844) reported that the general stated that 'all the other parts of the line are in good order, and the various bridges and other works, are highly creditable to Mr Jee and his assistants, as well as to the contractors and workmen'. He also noted that the Woodhead Tunnel was 'going on in a very satisfactory manner'. A special train left Glossop (i.e., Dinting) at twelve-noon, 'and soon arrived at Hadfield station, distant about 13 miles from Manchester'. Having 'stopped for a few moments' it then proceeded at 'a steady pace', with its whistle sounding continuously, making 'the beautiful vale of Longdendale, along which the line runs, echo with its shrill note.' The train arrived at Woodhead ('after a delightfully smooth passage') at 12.30 p.m., where the directors and their guests sat down to a 'sumptuous repast' in the new and extensive refreshment room at the Woodhead station. 'Nor were the workmen forgotten' and they dined in the open air on 'a plentiful supply of ale and bread and cheese'.

The fourth section of the line to open was that from Sheffield to Dunford Bridge – including the stations at Wadsley Bridge, Oughty Bridge, Deepcar, Wortley and Penistone – on 14 July 1845, without formalities. Penistone rapidly increased in importance with the opening of the Huddersfield & Sheffield Junction Railway, which joined the Woodhead route at Penistone. The SA&M had promoted this line and indeed had hoped to lease or purchase the route but this was not to be. In an astute tactical move to preserve its

Above: Hadfield station and goods shed, 3 May 1963.

Right: Hadfield over fifty years later, in summer 2016.

Every station needs a cat – Hadfield is no exception.

monopoly of trans-Pennine travel, the Manchester & Leeds acquired the line in 1846, despite the line's physical isolation from the remainder of the M&L network. It opened under the auspices of the Lancashire & Yorkshire Railway (as the M&L had become in July 1847) on 1 July 1850, the MS&L being granted running rights from the outset. A branch to Barnsley was opened in 1857 and a new station at Penistone was built in 1874.

Penistone was also the scene of one of the worst accidents in the history of the route at Bullhouse Bridge, 16 July 1884. The 12.30 p.m. express from Manchester London Road to London King's Cross passed through the Woodhead Tunnel at around 1.20 p.m. and was running downhill toward Penistone when the crank-axle of the locomotive broke close to the signal box for Bullhouses Colliery. Driver Sam Cawood immediately applied the brakes, the locomotive coming to rest 517 yards down the line. The train, consisting of eleven vehicles, however, left the rails and ten of them careered down the embankment. The *Illustrated London News* (26 July 1884) reported:

> A terrible railway accident, by which above twenty persons were killed and twice that number injured, took place on Wednesday week at Bullhouse Bridge, near Penistone, midway between Manchester and Sheffield. An express-train of the joint traffic system of the Manchester, Sheffield, and Lincolnshire and of the Great Northern Company, which had left Manchester at half-past twelve at noon, broke the axle of its engine, and the carriages behind were thrown from the bridge or embankment into the road below, a depth of about 16ft. They were turned upside down and broken, some were smashed to pieces, and half the passengers suffered, nineteen being taken dead out of the wreck of the train. Three others died after removal to Manchester. Among those killed were several

Site of the original 1840s station at Penistone.

The 1840s coal drops at Penistone.

Penistone Junction, *c.* 1900: MS&L/GC platforms on the left, Manchester & Leeds/Lancashire Yorkshire on the right.

Penistone today only sees one train an hour, running from Huddersfield to Sheffield via Barnsley.

38

The severity of the curve at Bullhouses is clearly depicted by the *Illustrated London News*.

1. The Part of the Train Which Fell Over the Embankment.—2. The Shattered Carriages Piled Up in the Road.—3. The Guard's Van.
E FATAL RAILWAY ACCIDENT AT BULLHOUSE BRIDGE, PENISTONE, NEAR SHEFFIELD

The Bullhouses crash was front-page news; the scale of the disaster is shown here by the *Graphic*.

ladies–Mrs. Coates, widow of a clergyman in Lancashire; Mrs. Stower and Mrs. Spencer, of Boston; Mrs. Edelstein, of New York; Miss Tetlow, of Bolton-by-Bolland; Mrs. Rawlings, of Redditch; and Mr and Mrs. Shorrock, of Darwen, who were on their way to a family wedding in London. Mr. Bromley, mechanical engineer, of Victoria-street, Westminster, and Mr. J. P. Woodhead, consulting engineer, of Manchester, were also killed. The Queen sent next day a message to the Mayor of Manchester, expressing her sympathy with those who are still suffering, and with the families of the dead.

The final death toll was twenty-four persons; the report of the HM Inspector of Railways, Major Marindin on 27 July included the inspection and testing of the crank axle on the locomotive and of sister locomotives, concluding that the breaking of the axle alone was not sufficient to cause the disaster; there had been 247 broken crank axles on the MS&L and none had caused a similar accident. Marindin noted that it was a combination of the broken axle – the wheels of which spread the track out of gauge – faulty couplings (leading to ten of the eleven vehicles breaking away) and the type of brake in use on the MS&L, the Smith vacuum brake. Once the carriages became disconnected from the locomotive and left the damaged rails, they naturally moved in a more-or-less straight line; in other words, down the embankment, rather than following the curve of the railway.

However, the biggest censure came for the brakes used by the MS&L. The Smith vacuum brake was a form of continuous (but not automatic) brake that was operated by the locomotive driver. An air pump, called an ejector, on the locomotive pumped air out of a sealed system, which allowed external air pressure to operate the vacuum cylinders on each vehicle to work the brakes. Each vehicle was connected to the locomotive by a flexible rubber hose. It was cheap to install and maintain, but had one serious fault: if the locomotive became detached from the train, or if the vacuum pipe developed a leak or was ruptured in any way, the brakes would stop working. Marindin noted,

> Now, while I do not believe that any brake which exists could have actually stopped the train on the falling gradient in the distance available, and could thus have averted the disaster, yet it is beyond question that a quickly-acting and powerful continuous-brake ought in this distance to have so reduced the speed that the consequences of the accident would probably have been far less fatal ... if the train had been fitted with an automatic-brake, which would have remained on when the parting took place, it is probable that four or five vehicles would, by its continued action and the consequent reduction of speed, have escaped with comparatively little damage.

Bullhouses Bridge, however, was not the first occasion that the Smith vacuum brake had failed to work on the MS&L:

> The value of a brake having rapid action, and above all, automatic action, in such a case as this, can hardly be contested; and although the Board of Trade has, as yet, no power to insist upon the adoption of a continuous-brake possessing these qualities, yet I would remind the Manchester, Sheffield and Lincolnshire Railway Company that this is the second emphatic warning which has been given to them within the last six months as to the need for automatic action in the brakes used upon their line; the previous instance

A rather mawkish postcard showing the wreckage at Bullhouses Bridge.

'Removing the victims to the Infirmary' – from the *Illustrated London News*.

41

being on the 6th February 1884, when after a carriage had left the rails when running at high speed near Dinting station, the vacuum-brake pipe was severed, the brake became useless, and the carriage was dragged along off the rails for over 350 yards further than it would have been if the brakes had remained on, at the imminent risk of falling, and taking with it the carriages behind it, over a viaduct 100 feet in height.

Even after this rebuke from the inspector, it took another three years and involvement from the Board of Trade before the MS&L fitted automatic vacuum brakes to their locomotives and rolling stock.

Opening Throughout

The final section, of course, was the Woodhead Tunnel, which was inspected by General Pasley on 20 December 1845. The entire route was formally opened on 22 December 1845. A special train left the Sheffield Bridgehouses at 10 a.m.

> Of about fifteen carriages, chiefly first class ... The train included such of the Directors and their friends that reside in Sheffield ... a union-jack floated from the engine and a band of music, belonging to the South-west Yorkshire Yeomanry Cavalry, occupied the first carriage. (*Manchester Courier*, 27 December 1845)

The train reached Woodhead at approximately 11 a.m. and arrived at Manchester London Road at 12.21 p.m., having 'stopped at several of the stations' en route, 'where additions were made to the party'. As the train entered London Road the band struck up 'See the Conquering Hero Comes' by Handel. Guests were received by the chairman, Mr John Parker MP, and, after a brief pause for refreshments, the train started for Sheffield at 1.32 p.m., being drawn by two locomotives 'under the direction of Mr Jee and Mr Purdon' As on its way to Manchester, the train stopped at several stations, including Newton and Glossop, to allow further passengers to embark. A 'long stoppage was made at the junction of the Glossop branch', where 'most of the gentlemen left the carriages and partly descended the hill to view the stupendous work, the Dinting viaduct'. The train reached Woodhead at 2.30 p.m., and Sheffield at 4.20 p.m. The guests and gathered company then made their way to the Cutler's Hall for a 'very handsome and substantial collation', which commenced at 5 p.m.; the *Manchester Courier* estimated some 230 persons sat down to dine. Guests included Lord Worsley; Edmund Buckley MP (Newcastle-under-Lyme); Henry Houldsworth, (chair of the Manchester & Leeds Railway); Mr J. P. Westhead (chair of the Manchester & Birmingham Railway); Joseph Locke ('who', the *Courier* was 'sorry to observe, was suffering from lameness, the effect of an accident of his gig') and the Mayors of Sheffield and Manchester. After the 'cloth was drawn' and the 'Non Nobis Domini' sung, the chairman gave in succession, 'The Queen', 'Prince Albert', 'The Queen Dowager and the Royal Family' and then the toast of the evening, 'Prosperity to the Sheffield, Ashton & Manchester Railway.' It appears to have been a particularly bibulous occasion; a further eight toasts were proposed: 'The Duke of Norfolk, the Earl of Scarborough, and the landowners on the line'; 'The Health of Mr Joseph Locke'; 'Lord Worsley, and our confederates in Lincolnshire,

Nottinghamshire and Yorkshire'; 'the health of Mr Houldsworth and the health of Mr Westhead'; 'Mr Jee, the resident engineer'; 'Mr Purdon, the engineer of the tunnel'; 'the Mayor of Manchester'; and finally 'the Chairman'. The meal concluded around 9 p.m. and those who had to travel back to Manchester and district withdrew in order to catch a special train at 9.30 p.m., which arrived at 11.45 p.m. No doubt there were a few sore heads in the morning.

Locomotives and Rolling Stock

The first three locomotives were supplied by Thomas Kirtley & Co. of Warrington in October and November 1841, costing £1,695 each. They were 0-4-2 locomotives of Stephenson's Large Samson type. A fourth locomotive (a 2-2-2 Patentee type) was supplied by Robert Stephenson & Co. in December of the same year, but the majority of locomotives – thirty-six of the forty-nine owned by the SA&M – were Manchester-built by Messrs. Sharp, Brothers & Co. (Sharp, Stewart from 1852). The largest single order for locomotives was for eighteen 2-2-2 tender engines with 5-foot driving wheels and 15 x 20 inch cylinders, from Sharp, Brothers & Co. for the opening of the line throughout in 1845. They were, according to the *Manchester Guardian,* fitted with 'patent steam expansions so that they can put on full or half steam', i.e., a form of expansion link valve gear, rather than gab gear. These 2-2-2s were converted to well tanks sometime before December 1856 after having been found to be unsuitable for working the heavily graded line, with double-heading usually having to be employed. They were succeeded by 0-6-0 locomotives from various manufacturers, including four by Sharp, Brothers & Co. All the locomotives were named and numbered, but the names were removed after 1860.

The SA&M had no locomotive works of its own, but repair shops were opened at Newton, under the superintendence of Richard Peacock. Peacock, born in Leeds and educated at Leeds Grammar School, had been a pupil of Daniel Gooch. At the precocious age of eighteen (in 1838), he had been appointed locomotive superintendent of the Leeds & Selby Railway, and joined the SA&M in 1841; he established Gorton Works in 1848. Inspired by his Unitarian faith, Peacock was a well-loved, liberal and philanthropic employer. He resigned from the SA&M in 1853 to found Beyer, Peacock of Gorton, Manchester, with Carl Beyer. Beyer had previously worked for Sharp Brothers. Peacock attended the Dissenting (latterly Unitarian) Chapel in Gorton and, as an act of thanksgiving for the recovery of his eldest daughter from typhoid fever, built a magnificent gothic church (Brookfield Church) for the congregation at the cost of £12,000. He paid for the peal of eight bells – each peal is named after his children – and donated the fine three-manual organ. He also paid for Brookfield Schools in Gorton (opened 1863), which was free from any religious test for admittance. He established a series of 'Free Sunday Evening Lectures' for his workers; was president of the Gorton & Openshaw Mechanics' Institute; patron of the 'Gorton Philharmonic Society'; a Justice of the Peace; and from 1885 to 1889 Liberal MP for Gorton. Peacock spent his entire life in Gorton living quite modestly at Gorton Hall; conversely Beyer purchased a country seat in North Wales at Llantisilio, in the Vale of Llangollen.

When the line first opened the number of carriages stood at fourteen: three first class, five second class and six third class vehicles. The first and second class carriages were

Above: *Sphynx*, a 0-6-0 heavy goods engine built for the SA&M by Messrs Sharp Brothers & Co. of Atlas Works, Manchester.

Left: Richard Peacock JP, MP (1820–1889); first and only SA&M locomotive superintendent (Brookfield Unitarian Church).

built by Messrs. Dunn & Son of Lancaster. The first class vehicles had three compartments, which sat six, and the press compared them very favourably with those of the Grand Junction Railway. The second class coaches were also of three compartments (which sat eight) and, like those of the Liverpool & Manchester, were open-sided, but boarded up at each end and the compartment divisions were carried up to the roof. The third class coaches were 'stand-ups' and lacked any seats or roofs. New coaching stock was delivered in 1845, with the *Sheffield Iris* newspaper calling them

> some of the of the most splendid carriages that ever adorned a line of Railway. To say nothing of the First and Second Class carriages, those of the Third Class are unparalleled for comfort and protection, being covered at the top and sides, and richly painted on the exterior. The guard box behind is sheltered on three sides and the top so that even in the coldest season, this important functionary will be protected from the inclemency of the weather.

The carriages were probably painted green and were adorned with the names and coats of arms of Sheffield, Ashton-under-Lyne and Manchester. The third class vehicles were 14 feet long, 6 feet 6 inches wide and 5 feet 3 inches high, and able to accommodate about thirty passengers.

The magnificent Brookfield Church, built by Richard Peacock, and where he and his family are interred in the family mausoleum.

Chapter 3

Terminal Stations

Manchester

The Manchester & Birmingham Railway opened its temporary terminus in Travis Street in May 1840 with the opening of their line to Stockport. The M&B had been conceived back in 1836 by a group of wealthy Manchester businessmen as a more direct route between Manchester and Birmingham, avoiding the longer Grand Junction route via Newton Junction on the Liverpool & Manchester. It was to join the Grand Junction at Crewe, and trains would be taken on by that company to Birmingham, but worked back by the M&B. The chairman was Thomas Ashton of Hyde, a wealthy Unitarian mill owner and philanthropist. It was incorporated in 1837 and opened in stages between 1840 and 1842. Its most famous engineering work is the massive twenty-seven-arch Stockport Viaduct, built at a cost of £70,000 and using 11 million bricks.

The *Manchester Courier* (6 June 1840) described the temporary station as being 'convenient' and

> formed under three of the arches ... the space obtained will be amply sufficient for the purposes of the company ... Entering the station by a door on the side of the arches next Fairfield-street, the passengers ascend to the line by means of a temporary wooden staircase, which is erected outside the arches, and inclosed; and walking a few yards forward, they find the carriages drawn up, ready for their reception.

One of the most admired engineering aspects of the line into Manchester was the iron skew bridge over Fairfield Street, set at an angle of 24.5 degrees; its span was 128 feet 9 inches but 'the square span of the street is not more than 48 feet'. The cast-iron parapets featured shields bearing the arms of the M&B and the inscription 'Manchester and Birmingham Railway 1839'. When this bridge was dismantled, the decorative panels were recovered and are now part of the National Collection.

The SA&M was granted running rights into the new station via a junction at Ardwick from March 1841, but they were obliged to pay for the upkeep of the track and viaduct from Chancery Lane Junction to Store Street; the M&B were also empowered to charge 2*d*

The main façade at Store Street, a.k.a., London Road station, in the 1840s. (*Illustrated London News*)

The iron skew bridge, carrying the Manchester & Birmingham/SA&M line over Fairfield Street.

per passenger and 3*d* per ton of freight passing over the line into the station. The directors' meeting reported in February 1842 that the new joint station on Store Street was rapidly approaching completion:

> The approach from Ducie-street is completed, except the parapets and paving of the road and footpaths. All the vaulting between Store-street and Ashton-street constituting the site of the station is erected; nearly the whole of the station is ballasted; the foundation of the turntables and other parts of the superstructure are laid. The walls of the engine house are built to the height of four feet above the level of the rails. The booking-offices are advancing rapidly. The two bridges over Ashton-street and the arches of the viaduct between Ashton-street and the present temporary station ... will be turned in three weeks from this time. Nearly all the iron work for the roofing is prepared ... (*Manchester Courier*, 26 February 1842)

Store Street was opened with little fanfare on Tuesday 10 May 1842. It was officially renamed London Road in 1847, although newspapers had been referring to it as 'London Road' from its opening, so perhaps the name change brought it into line with popular usage. The *Manchester Courier* (12 May 1842) described the new building:

> The new station ... is erected on a viaduct of sixteen arches, 238 feet long, 34 feet span, rising to the height of 30 feet above London-Road. These arches are fitted up as warehouses for the parties who have arranged with the company for the conveyance of merchandize along the line. The approach to the passenger station is by an incline from Ducie-Street. Facing the approach, at the top of the incline, is a beautiful stone building, in the Italian style of architecture, which forms the prominent feature of the station ... Turning to the left, the visitor approaches a range of buildings 500 feet long, containing the booking offices, waiting rooms, parcels offices, &c., which are particularly spacious and convenient; over these, and connected by a corridor extending the whole length, are the proprietor's meeting rooms, directors' and treasurer's rooms, manager's and engineer's rooms, and the offices for the various clerks of the company.

The new station had only two platforms – arrival and departure:

> Passing through the booking offices, he will arrive on a platform for passengers on departure. This is 500 feet in length, and 12 feet wide, the platform floor being laid with asphalt: this platform, together with the two departure lines of rails, is covered with a light iron roof, 480 feet long, and 34 feet span. On the opposite side of the station is the platform for the arrival lines, 312 feet long and 12 feet wide, beyond which again is a spacious area for carriages waiting the arrival of passengers. This is paved with wooden blocks ... between the platform are six lines of rails connected with three rows of turntables; four of these lines are connected with a turntable, thirty feet in diameter, so arranged as to turn an engine and tender at once ... this part of the station is covered with an iron roof, 212 feet long, in two spans of 52 feet 6 inches, and 34 respectively.

The massive brick-built goods warehouse on Ducie Street; now the Palace Hotel and originally linked by viaduct to London Road station.

In addition to the approach ramp from Ducie Street was

> A double stair-case of peculiar construction, for the accommodation of passengers, so arranged that persons arriving ascend by one flight of steps, the entrance to which is in London-road; whilst those departing descend by a separate flight of steps into Store-street.

Goods facilities were provided by a massive brick-built warehouse on the north-eastern side of the site. George Clarke Pauling of Manchester built it in just under twelve months (work commenced 12 June 1841), using 'twenty three million bricks ... and 800 tons of cast iron.'

Through Running

As early as 1838 the SA&M had proposed a physical connection with the Liverpool & Manchester, but the latter company declined. Almost as soon as London Road had been opened, however, both the Manchester & Birmingham and the SA&M once again contemplated through running to the L&M at Liverpool Road and with the Manchester & Leeds at Oldham Street. At a directors' meeting held in Manchester on 24 February

49

1842 they proposed forming a junction with the Manchester & Leeds at Oldham Street, which 'would be most advantageous' to both companies. Duly an application was made to Parliament for an Enabling Act; the cost of the junction was estimated in September 1842 to be some £66,500.

The threat of constructing the junction between the M&L and M&B spurred the directors of the L&M into action; they proposed a 'central junction of railways' at Ordsall Lane, where lines would diverge to the north to Hunt's Bank for the M&L, and via the 'Southern Junction Line' to link with the M&B at Store Street. The L&M directors also proposed leasing their entire line to the M&L, but the latter demanded that any such lease be 'contingent on the defeat of any opposition line of railway that might be projected between Liverpool and Manchester'. Despite an offer from the L&M of a 10 per cent guarantee, the proposal failed. One major problem of through running from the L&M onto the M&L was the matter of gauge: the L&M was built at 'standard gauge' while the M&L was half an inch wider, at 4 feet 9 inches. The M&B was also built to a gauge of 4 feet 9 while the SA&M was standard gauge. The L&M extension to Hunts Bank was engineered by Edward Woods and was opened in May 1844.

The M&B extension to Hunts Bank was effectively a non-starter; the junction was to be made by a 1,000-yard-long tunnel but there would have been a difference of 16 feet between

Road, rail and canal meet at Deansgate/Whitworth Street; the elegant cast-iron bridges carrying the MSJ&A over the Rochdale Canal and onwards to its junction with the LNWR at Ordsall Lane.

Knott Mill, a.k.a. Deansgate station, built by the MSJ&A in the 1890s, replacing the original timber structure of 1848.

the two lines, making through running an impossibility. Success of the L&M extension to Hunts Bank led the SA&M and the M&B to jointly promote the 'South Junction line' (as proposed back in 1842 by the L&M) that became the 'Manchester South Junction & Altrincham Railway,' which was primarily designed to give the two sponsoring lines the much-needed communication with the L&M. The Act received Royal Assent on 21 July 1845, the engineer being Joseph Locke. The project stalled, however, for want of money and a second Act (22 July 1848) was required to raise the additional funds to complete the work. The first section, 1 ¾ miles from London Road to Ordsall Lane, opened in July 1849 but not without accident: one of the arches of the viaduct on Oxford Road collapsed on 20 January 1849 as the shuttering was removed, killing two men and injuring three more. Two more arches collapsed five days later; the slow setting of mortar in cold, wet weather was the official cause for the collapse.

The Manchester, Sheffield & Lincolnshire Railway

In 1844, the M&B, goaded by George Hudson (one of its directors) and 'aided and abetted by the Midland Railway', proposed that they should jointly lease the SA&M; the Midland readily agreed to the proposal as it offered them a more direct route to Manchester. The terms offered were accepted by the Board of the SA&M, and a special meeting of the proprietors was called to confirm them. The M&L, however, got wind of the proposal and at the eleventh hour sent their own counter offer on slightly better terms. Despite this, the SA&M Board agreed to the lease of their line by the M&B and MR at a special meeting on 4 November 1844, and a Bill was duly deposited to Parliament. Six months later, however, this agreement was nullified by the SA&M shareholders on 15 April 1845 because the M&B was becoming closely associated with the London & Birmingham Railway – 'a development not at all to their liking.'

After their failure to lease their line, the Board of the SA&M began overtures, which would eventually establish the Woodhead Route as part of a coast–coast and London railway. Their first act was to amalgamate with the Barnsley Junction Railway in September 1845. During the following year, negotiations opened with the Sheffield & Lincolnshire Junction Railway (opened 1849) and the Great Grimsby & Sheffield Junction Railway. These were to be absorbed by the new Manchester, Sheffield & Lincolnshire Railway by an Act of 27 July 1846. The new railway came into being on 11 January 1847; in the same year the Manchester & Lincoln Union Railway was also absorbed. The route opened throughout, from Manchester to Grimsby and New Holland in July 1849. Finally, by a Consolidation Act of 1 August 1849, all the component companies were dissolved and re-incorporated as the Manchester, Sheffield & Lincolnshire Railway.

Trains to the South

The first through trains to London were run by the Great Northern Railway to Sheffield in 1851. In the summer of 1857 the MS&L came to an agreement with the GNR over running rights, and from 1 October of that year trains began to run from Manchester, via Sheffield and Retford, to King's Cross in five hours. Tickets cost the princely sum of 35s first class, 25s second class, and 15s 8d third class. Seven trains were run during weekdays and four on Sundays. This was two shillings cheaper than the London & North Western Railway (LNWR), who were offering a first class fare to London of 37s, but only 17s second class; third class was not catered for. This led to increasing tension between the MS&L and the LNWR, especially at London Road. It was reported that men of the LNWR would place obstacles on the track to prevent MS&L trains from entering London Road; MS&L clerks were turned out of their offices and, according to the Counsel of the MS&L, Mr Denison QC, the LWNR had

> Beg[u]n to take people into custody for coming by the Sheffield trains into the Manchester station; they frightened an old lady out of her wits, and distracted several feeble people; but at last they got hold of a lawyer who showed them they had caught a tartar; and so after that no more passengers were apprehended. We [the MS&L] had painted our names up over our shop, but they, being in possession, which is nine points of the law, swept them out with their brush. They kept a truck standing in front of the platform and left timber trains in front of our express trains. They turned our clerks out of the booking office – indeed they nailed up the part which the Sheffield Company had been accustomed to use. (Dow: 1945, pp. 41–42)

Fire, Rebuilding and Expansion

It was against this acrimonious background that the two companies declared an uneasy truce in 1859 in order to rebuild London Road; having only two platforms presented considerable operational bottlenecks and the new station would provide separate platforms for both the MS&L (Platforms A and B) and the LNWR. This would solve, in theory, the repeated disputes between both companies.

The decision to rebuild might have been inspired by a disastrous fire at London Road in November 1854, which caused over £1,000 of damage to the buildings. The fire was believed to have started in the cashier's office of the MS&L end of the building and from there 'ran from office to office with alarming rapidity' down the length of the entire departure side of the station. 'Every exertion was made by the firemen to check the progress of the fire' but their efforts were 'thrown into confusion' by trains, which continued to attempt to arrive at the station. Moreover, there was a serious shortage of water – and water pressure – for the fire pumps – and the firemen laboured from 10.20 p.m. to 1 a.m. the following morning to extinguish the fire. The roofs and contents of the entire range of buildings were destroyed; the MS&L had sensibly insured their premises, via the Scottish Insurance Union, but the LNWR, it was found, was uninsured.

The *Manchester Courier* announced on 2 November 1861 that plans for the new station had been finalised; a new goods station in Ducie Street was to be built and the existing MS&L grain warehouses were to be demolished. The approach ramp was to be widened, as was the railway viaduct as far as Ardwick Junction. The *Courier* opined that the 1851 buildings were

> Dingy, disgraceful and dangerous platform and offices which many a fiftieth-rate country town would have blushed to recognise within its confines ...

The old station complex was to be demolished and replaced by a 'handsome Italianate structure', 200 feet wide, 162 feet deep and over 70 feet tall. Booking offices and platforms (240 yards long) for the LNWR were to be on the right and those of the MS&L on the left; both companies were to have 'a perfectly distinct set of lines for arriving and departing trains; as indeed will be the case from the Ardwick Junction'. The major architectural feature of the new building was to be a 'noble hall', 64 feet long, 31 feet wide and 70 feet high, 'lit from the roof.' The contracts for the new building were let by May 1862; Messrs. W. and H. Southern of Salford were the principal contractors, with Messrs. Patterson of Manchester being responsible for the stonework and E. T. Bellhouse of Manchester the iron work, with the brickwork by Mr Rutherford. The contracts stipulated that the building was to be roofed by June 1863. A new glass and iron overall roof for the train shed was to be built: 625 feet long, of two spans with an overall width of 192 feet 6 inches. It was supported on twenty-seven massive cast-iron columns, 27 feet long, the whole roof rising to a height of 64 feet from rail level. The roof was eight bays long; the first six being 78 feet wide, while the remaining two (furthest away from the main building) were 88 feet wide.

The building was roofed and was being fitted out by November 1864; the *Manchester Times* (12 November 1864) thought that the new building would come into use by Christmas. New warehouses for the MS&L were erected, as well as extensive new stables

The imposing façade of the 1861–65 London Road station, pictured in the late 1880s.

View from the footbridge at London Road, looking back toward the booking halls, etc.: MS&L Platforms (A–C) are on the right and LNWR on the left. Note the fence dividing the two companies' property!

on the site of the former MS&L grain warehouses. A new goods viaduct was built along Broad Street. Ducie Street was to be widened and re-routed to form a junction with Piccadilly 'instead of the old, narrow and dangerous circuit'; London Road was widened and Sheffield Street 'completely covered over' by the enlarged station complex. Tragically, while the new train shed roof was being completed, it partially collapsed on 22 January 1866 at around 1.45 p.m. Two men (Thomas Garton Sherwood and Mark Russell, both thirty-five) working on the structure were killed and a further thirty-one were injured. The ironwork for the full eight bays had been erected, and they were in the process of being glazed when the seventh bay of the roof collapsed; '88 feet in length, and two spans wide, fell with a tremendous crash into the station.' Standing under the new roof was the 1.45 p.m. train to Buxton:

> This train, only a few moments before was exactly under that portion of roof which fell … most fortunately, the driver shunted a few yards backward, and when the roof fell in only a few timbers and slates alighted on the engine. The driver had a very narrow escape … One engine, with three or four carriages, was standing exactly underneath that portion of the arch which fell on the right-hand side of the station (nearest to Birmingham Street), and it was perfectly miraculous how the driver escaped instant death. The engine was completely covered in *débris*, and the driver would have unquestionably been killed had he not thrown himself on the platform of the engine. (*Manchester Courier*, 27 January 1866)

Two men were left stranded on the roof and 'ladders were immediately fetched' to rescue them but two bricklayers, upon seeing the iron work coming down, jumped off, falling 30 feet to street level. The wounded and injured were rushed to the Manchester Infirmary in cabs. Traffic on the MS&L and LNWR was partially suspended, the former forwarding their passengers to Ardwick by cabs. By 5 p.m., the debris had been cleared and the station was able to re-open. The damage to the roof and the building was estimated to be in the region of £6,000. On the following day (Tuesday 23) the remaining sections of the damaged eighth bay were demolished: the damaged sections were unbolted from the remainder of the roof and pulled down using 'two powerful locomotives', leaving the other seven bays still standing. It was estimated that, 'At present about four-fifths of the new passenger shed has been left available to both companies'. 'So rapid' was the work in 'clearing away the ruins of the portion of the roof which was taken down on Tuesday night' that, by 3 p.m. on the Wednesday, the passenger station was re-opened and repairs were begun in earnest. A full inspection was carried out by Captain Tyler, HM Inspector of Railways, which concluded that one of the iron beams had failed due to being overloaded from the weight of contractor's equipment, scaffolding, and the workmen themselves. Flaws in the design were also highlighted, including the use of cast-iron supports at either end of the wrought-iron beams.

The station was enlarged again from 1879 to 1881 on the LNWR side when two additional roof spans were erected, one measuring 80 feet and the other 70 feet, bringing the total width of the platform area to 334 feet. The existing platforms were all lengthened to nearly 800 feet and the total cost, including the purchase of land, was £300,000. There were now two LNWR departure platforms and two arrival platforms, divided by two carriage roads. The MS&L provision was increased to three platforms – A, B, and C to

The revamped 2002 building at Manchester Piccadilly in summer 2016. It was built ahead of the Commonwealth Games, replacing a singularly ugly concrete box.

differentiate them from the LWNR. The extension was supported on massive cast-iron columns and the undercroft thus created was used as additional goods storage, linked to rail level via hydraulic cranes. New platforms for the Manchester, South Junction & Altrincham were also provided.

Sheffield Stations

Unlike in Manchester, the SA&M had their own station in Sheffield; originally located at Bridgehouses, approached by Nursery Street. Originally it only had a single platform – typical of the period – for arrival and departure.

Proposals for a new station in Sheffield were raised as early as 1845, but it was only with the formation of the MS&L that the proposals took the form of stone and mortar. In order to carry the new line toward Lincolnshire, a new viaduct known as the 'Wicker Arches' was constructed immediately to the east of Bridgehouses station. The new viaduct was some 660 yards long and cost £80,000, crossing the River Wicker by a 'magnificent arch of 72 feet span.' The *Sheffield Independent* (7 October 1848) noted

> It is about 700 yards length, extending from the present station in Clay Gardens, through the Nursery, across the Wicker road, over the river, the site of the old Blonk Dam, the

yard of the Sheaf Works, and the canal, having its abutment on the hill-side on the east side of the Canal ... on the east side of the canal there are six flat segmental arches, two of them being of 50, and the others of 47 feet span ... the piers are most massive and beautiful masonry. Their strength is enormous. They have rather an appearance to sustain a bombardment ... the arches are of brickwork faced with stone ...

Sadly, during February 1848 a moveable crane and some of the scaffolding collapsed, killing four men, and in October one of the arches collapsed but without any loss of life. The viaduct was opened on 16 December 1848 when the first train passed over it.

The new Sheffield Station – named Victoria in honour of the young Queen – was opened on Monday 15 September 1851; it occupied 'the space from the Wicker Viaduct to the Canal, crossing the river, the site of the old Blonk Dam, the Cattle Market and Fair Ground, and the back of the Sheaf Works...'

The new building was faced with hammer-dressed Greenmoor Stone, and supported on a massive viaduct 40 feet above the level of the Wicker. The new station was

Gaily decorated with flags, some bearing loyal inscriptions, and others with wishes for the prosperity of the railway ... while many more were simply national types, or decorative banners. (*Sheffield Independent* 20 September 1851)

The same newspaper described the station as having

A commanding aspect, and one though its front is destitute or ornament, being very simple in its architectural character, it appears to us infinitely more appropriate for a place of business, belonging to proprietors who have yet to make a large concern pay,

Sheffield Victoria station and Royal Hotel, photographed *c.* 1900.

than the more pretentious and ornate stations in which some companies have indulged themselves. The station is approached from Blonk Street by a straight incline, built upon arches, which is 50 feet wide and 320 yards long ... As it approaches the front of the station it opens out into an extended and ample area.

The Station consists of a centre and wings, the latter being extended by a high fence wall ... the length of the masonry frontage is 400 feet. The station is built of rock-faced Greenmoor stone ... and facings of ashlar from Wadsley ... the front of the station is admired by those who are judges of such work, as surpassing in excellence any previous specimens. (*Sheffield Independent* 13 September 1851)

Passengers were protected from the elements by a 'covered verandah, with glazed roof supported by iron brackets'. The main entrance, or waiting hall, occupied the central section of the building: it measured 50 feet by 30 feet and 25 feet high. There was an 'enclosed area' for the booking clerks; the central window for first class passengers; the left hand for Great Northern passengers; and the right hand for second and third class passengers on the MS&L. The eastern wing of the building comprised 'refreshment and waiting rooms, conveniences, parcels office and on the chamber floor, the station master's house.' In the western wing were the telegraph office, stationmaster's office, and 'rooms for lamps, porters, guards &c. and the engineer's office'. Above them were administrative offices.

The station had four running roads – 'two will be used by trains passing through the station. The other two will be occupied by spare carriages.' Goods trains 'will not pass through the station at all. Two lines of rails are provided for them outside the north-eastern wall of the railway station, and they will run past without coming in the way at all of the passenger traffic.'

There was a single departure/arrival platform for through trains, 1,000 feet long and 40 feet wide, and at either end two bay platforms. The *Sheffield Independent* described their curious operation:

When a train comes in from the west, with some passengers for the eastern line and the Midland, carriages for the Midland passengers will stand in the western dock [i.e., bay] side by side with the train just arrived, but separated from it by a narrow platform. Across this platform, the Midland passengers and their luggage will be very easily transferred to their particular carriages, and when the main train for the east is gone, the train to join the Midland will be ready to back out of the dock and follow. So on the other side. The trains from the Midland run into the dock where such passengers as are going westward will be transferred to the through train standing by the side of their own train within a few feet of it. (*Sheffield Independent*, 13 September 1851)

The platforms were covered by a glass and iron roof, 400 feet long and 83 feet wide, 'covering an area of 34,600 superficial square feet'. The 'light and airy appearance of the structure' was 'very pleasing'. During 1862 the Royal Victoria Hotel was opened on the station approach and, during 1899 and 1900, three additional platforms (numbered 1, 2 and 5) were added.

Sheffield Victoria, following its facelift of 1939, with Art Deco style replacing heavy Victorian.

Sheffield Victoria was demolished in 1989, but platforms and some track remain *in situ.*

Chapter 4

The Twentieth Century – Modernisation and Electrification

The MS&L, under the dynamic leadership of Edward Watkin, was transformed from a simple trans-Pennine route with the opening of its 'London Extension' to London Marylebone in 1899. To mark this transition, the company was re-named as the Great Central Railway in 1897. The Woodhead Route became a key component of north–south expresses. In 1907 the Great Central quadrupled the line between Hadfield and Woodhead, despite opposition from Derbyshire County Council.

The Woodhead Tunnel has always been susceptible to extreme weather; during an unseasonably wet August in 1900 the line was completely blocked near Crowden

> To a height of ten feet, huge boulders of every conceivable shape and size, intermingled with shrubs, were piled up … it had all happened in an instant … A cloudburst in the hills had caused the water to rush down in a terrific torrent, tearing with it boulders, fences, trees, and shrubs. Not being able to pass under the culverts, it tore down the stone wall bordering on the railway track, and swept with indescribable force over the lines, there depositing huge boulders and tearing up sleepers and rails. (*Manchester Courier*, 7 August 1900)

Luckily, the driver of the 3.30 p.m. Manchester–Sheffield express had seen the landslip and immediately applied his brakes. He then 'intended on returning to Hadfield' but 'the cloud-burst had occasioned a similar accident of even worse a character 500 yards in our rear' leaving the train and its passengers stranded. The passengers 'made themselves as comfortable as [they] could' in the carriages while 'outside it rained harder than ever'. After five hours the rain had 'diminished in breadth', allowing some plucky male passengers – fortified by some whisky – to clamber over the landslip behind the train and head towards Crowden station, and in so doing found a further four trains stranded behind the landslip. The passengers were finally evacuated and spent the night at Crowden station; some of

An early colour postcard of a Great Central Express from Manchester to Marylebone, near Hadfield.

their number decided on the following morning to walk to Penistone – a 12-mile walk in the rain – to find breakfast and to catch a London train. The blocking of the line led to disappointment for the townsfolk of Denton, whose band had won a silver cup (valued at £1,000) at the Crystal Palace Band Contest. The cup was being brought from London by train and, 'owing to the flooding of the Woodhead Tunnel', did not arrive for the formal presentation but did arrive 'very late at night' and was immediately 'lodged in the strong room of the bank.'

Perhaps one of the most gruesome discoveries in the tunnel was the 'find of a body on the buffers' of a locomotive at Sheffield Victoria on 11 July 1925. The body was that of one John Scaife of Oldham. A second body was discovered a week later on the morning of 18 July 1925 at Penistone of an unknown 'man who had rode on top of the train' and had presumably fallen from his precarious perch. Four years later a fireman, Walter Danson of Pickering, was killed at the Dunford Bridge end of the tunnel in March 1929 because he 'did not see the headlights' of an oncoming train. Indeed, there was a suspicion that the headlights had in fact been extinguished 'by the dense atmosphere in the tunnel'. The same 'dense atmosphere' had, twenty years earlier, lead to the 'poisoning' of 'several of the Stockport County players'. The *Sheffield Evening Telegraph* (10 October 1905) reported that two of the players – Messrs. Heywood and Dodd – were 'suffering from the effects of the sulphur fumes which pervaded the atmosphere near Woodhead' and were unable to take to the field in a forthcoming match.

In February 1936 the 4.55 p.m. from Marylebone to Manchester London Road became stranded in the tunnel for nearly two hours when the locomotive failed. Some of the

61

passengers reported hearing 'a knocking sound for some time and then in the tunnel the train suddenly came to a standstill', while another thought 'a piece of the engine had fallen out'. A relief engine was sent from Dunford bridge but, because the 'heating went off' in the carriages, the passengers had to spend an hour and a half 'freezing cold'. Despite this many of them went to sleep in their compartments. The train finally arrived at Manchester at 11.45 p.m., rather than the timetabled 9.00 p.m.. In the September of the same year, the line was blocked due to a 'heavy rock fall' in the Woodhead Tunnel, while permanent way staff was clearing debris 'from a collision between two goods trains the day before'. *The Yorkshire Post* (25 September 1936) reported that a goods train passing through the tunnel had 'broken in two' and

> Part of the trucks ran backwards into the tunnel. They came into collision with another train in the tunnel and the wagons were piled up almost to the roof of the tunnel.

While the breakdown team were clearing the debris on the following day, 'rocks began to fall' from the tunnel roof, 'causing no injury', but 'the foreman of the Gorton Locomotive Shed, Manchester, a man named Maughan' who was in the tunnel was 'overcome by fumes from the goods engine which had been involved in the previous days' smash.' It was the second fall of the roof that resulted in the death of one Maurice Clarke of Denton and the wounding of nine of his colleagues, three of them (Thomas Rugman, Frank Whalley and Harry Cook) severely. One eyewitness saw 'Three men were partially buried, and others knocked down' in the collapse. Ambulances were called from Hyde and Glossop and, according to *The Yorkshire Post* (26 September 1936), all together some forty men 'had

Another early colour postcard of a GC Express, from Sheffield to Manchester.

a narrow escape'. A verdict of 'death by misadventure' was recorded. Despite the LNER stating that the tunnel was perfectly safe, part of the roof had collapsed a year earlier in July 1935, thankfully without any injury.

Modernisation

In order to improve safety in the tunnel, the Great Central Railway introduced an automatic signal box mid-way along its length, dividing the tunnel into two sections. The new signal box was pneumatically operated and was considered a great boon to traffic on the line:

> Underground Railway Signalling ... The Great Central Railway, in order to accelerate main line traffic, have just completed a contract with British Pneumatic Railway Signalling Company for the installation of automatic pneumatic signalling ... owing to the impossibility of manning a signal box in so unfavourable an underground position ... Woodhead Tunnel, over three miles in length, has to be worked as a single block section, main line expresses being consequentially greatly impeded ... by dividing the line into sections ... will accelerate express traffic between Manchester, Sheffield, and London ... (*Sheffield Daily Telegraph,* 8 December 1902)

The new signal box and 'signalling arrangements' came into use in February 1903. At the same time it was proposed to supplement the 'existing semaphore signal with the Miller Visible Engine Signal', installed in the cab of every locomotive, which worked in conjunction with an electric track circuit, similar to that used on the GWR. An 'experimental installation' at the entrance to the Woodhead Tunnel was installed by the British Miller Signal Co. for trials by the Great Central. The Miller system was an American innovation, having been first introduced on the New York Central, and was 'said to have given every satisfaction'.

Ventilation of the tunnel was improved by the Great Central between 1912 and 1915, involving the widening of the five ventilation shafts and lining them with brick. The work took place 'from the surface, a strong steel scaffold being suspended on plugs driven in the shaft sides to carry the excavated material.' The *Sheffield Evening Telegraph* remarked 'The undertaking was carried out without a single accident.'

Electrification

The Great Central first proposed electrification of the Manchester–Sheffield services, and the idea was taken up again by the LNER in 1926, reporting on the desirability – and feasibility – of the scheme in 1929. *The Sheffield Daily Independent* (4 January 1929) reported:

> It is the existence of the Woodhead Tunnel ... that has made it necessary to think out some scheme for changing the system of transport on the L.N.E.R. The tunnel has long been a source of worry to railway officials ... it is impossible under the present steam-engine system, to speed it up in the tunnel itself. Only one train is allowed in the tunnel at once,

EM2 No. 27001 *Ariadne* prepares to depart Manchester Piccadilly with a train to Sheffield. She is now preserved at MSI, Manchester.

EM2 No. 27006 *Pandora* departing Manchester Piccadilly for Sheffield Victoria.

and as it takes a passenger train six minutes to pass through, a maximum of only ten trains an hour can pass through it ... The advantage of the electric trains is ... that they could run closer together on the line, with the result that more trains an hour could be got through the tunnel.

The exact form of electrification had not been decided upon; the newspapers reporting that third-rail electrification was the preferred option rather than overhead due to the presence of the Woodhead Tunnel. Electrification would be restricted to the main lines, with shunting and yard work carried out by steam. The LNER and LMS carried out trials of a 1,500-v DC overhead system on the MSJ&A between Manchester and Altrincham in 1930. The Wier Report of 1931, commissioned in the interests of standardisation, recommended that future electrification, other than on the Southern, which used 750-v DC third rail, was to be 1,500-v DC overhead. Five years later the electrification of the Manchester–Sheffield electrification was resurrected – with considerable Government assistance – and the LNER estimated a cost of £2.5 million. Electrified branches to Manchester Central via Fallowfield, to Ashton Park Parade, Glossop, and Wath were proposed. Work was abruptly halted in 1939 due to the outbreak of war. *The Yorkshire Post* in December 1939 reported that by the time when work was suspended:

> About half the civil engineering work has been completed, several miles of structures to carry 1,500-volt transmission wires have been erected, special over-head equipment is being installed in the Woodhead Tunnel, and work is well-advanced on a steam and electric locomotive depot at Darnall, Sheffield.

A committee was appointed in 1944 to review the electrification scheme, suggesting additional engine-changeover facilities at Sheffield Victoria, a new repair depot at Reddish (on the branch from Fairfield Junction to Manchester Central) rather than at Gorton, the opening-out of the Thurgoland Tunnel, and the use of colour light signalling.

Heavy maintenance was carried out 1946/47, with both bores being closed for separate periods of nine months, during which time some traffic was diverted over LMS routes. This lead to considerable congestion around Manchester and the Yorkshire Coalfields, causing coal shortages in the south. To make matters worse, the tunnel was blocked and all traffic suspended for several days in April 1947, when five goods wagons derailed at the eastern end of the Woodhead Tunnel.

In 1946 the LNER Board was faced with having two tunnels on a strategic rail route that were nearing the end of their working lives; abandonment of the Victorian tunnels and the construction of a new one seemed the only practical solution. Three different schemes were proposed: 1) a new single-line tunnel and a repair of an existing tunnel; 2) two new single-line tunnels or 3) a new double-line tunnel. The latter proposition was recommended by the civil engineer of the LNER and adopted by the Board. Parliamentary powers were obtained via the LNER Act of 1947, authorising the new twin-bore tunnel at Woodhead and a new double-track tunnel at Thurgoland. The new tunnels were required because they lacked sufficient clearance for the new over-head (despite equipment being installed in the old Woodhead bores before the war). But all was not doom and gloom: *The Yorkshire Evening Post* triumphantly announced on 20 August 1947 a

£6,000,000 Rail Electrification … work is to be resumed at once on the L.N.E.R. plan to electrify the line between Wath, Sheffield and Manchester … the scheme will cost about £6,000,000. When completed, it is estimated there will be an annual saving of 100,000 tons of coal. Faster passenger and freight services will follow. A total of 75 miles will be electrified … the L.N.E.R. stated to-day that practically 50 per cent of the civil engineering work has been done, and orders placed for rolling stock and electrical equipment for locomotives.

The new tunnel was estimated to cost £2,800,000. Mr J. I. C. Campbell, the LNER's civil engineer, was appointed to superintend the construction through to completion. Messrs. Balfour, Beatty were appointed as contractors. Unlike the old tunnels, the new tunnel would rise at 1:129 from the Woodhead end for 2 miles and then fall at 1:1,186 toward Dunford Bridge, which in theory would allow two trains to work through the tunnel simultaneously. Work commenced in the spring of 1949 and, unlike a century earlier, attention was paid to the wellbeing of the tunnel workers, which included a 'well-equipped camp with canteens, cinema, sick bay, post office and other amenities' at Dunford Bridge. On completion of the work, the cinema and sewerage plant were gifted to the local community. Spoil was removed by two narrow-gauge (2-foot gauge) tracks, operated by battery-electric locomotives.

The 467-foot-deep pilot shaft began in autumn 1949 and the pilot tunnel from Dunford Bridge met the pilot shaft in April 1951, completing the eastern half of the tunnel. The western or Woodhead end of the tunnel was completed on May 16 1951 when Mr J. C. L. Train, formerly chief civil engineer of the LNER and latterly member of the Railway Executive for Civil Engineering, detonated the final charge. The tunnel was lined with concrete 6 feet thick, laid using a special travelling shutter. Track laying – using pre-fabricated panels laid by a special track-laying machine – in the new tunnel was completed on 3 September 1953, involving 1,000 tons of rail, 13,000 sleepers and 20,000 tons of ballast. Some six men died during construction of the tunnel.

While the new tunnels were being dug, 'the first aim was the completion and inauguration of electric equipment and traction on the busy … Wath-Penistone-Dunford Bridge section', a heavily graded (the ruling gradient was 1:40) section of line, which in LNER days had been worked by the six-cylinder Beyer, Garrett locomotive of 1925. The Wath–Dunford Bridge section was opened for traffic on 4 February 1952 with freights trains worked by two EM1 locomotives. The second section to be opened was from London Road to Glossop, Reddish depot and the spur to Ashton Moss freight yard. It was opened throughout 14 June 1953. Electric multiple units worked the local passenger services to Glossop and Hadfield. The final section, Penistone–Sheffield, was inaugurated 20 September 1954. Two years later, however, British Railways took the decision that would render the Woodhead Route isolated and obsolete by recommending that all future electrification would be 25,000-v AC. In March 1956 the British Transport Commission recommended that all future electrification should be 25,000-v AC, a decision largely based on the relative expense between AC and DC electrification. AC required lighter overhead equipment, fewer sub-stations and less civil engineering, and it was possible to supply 25,000-v AC at fifty cycles directly from the national grid. For example, BR estimated that the electrification of the Euston–Manchester route with DC would have required seventy sub-stations, the raising of over half of the 904 bridges on the route, and enlargement of tunnels at a cost of £38.6 million; the cost with AC was £29.3 million, which was not an inconsiderable saving.

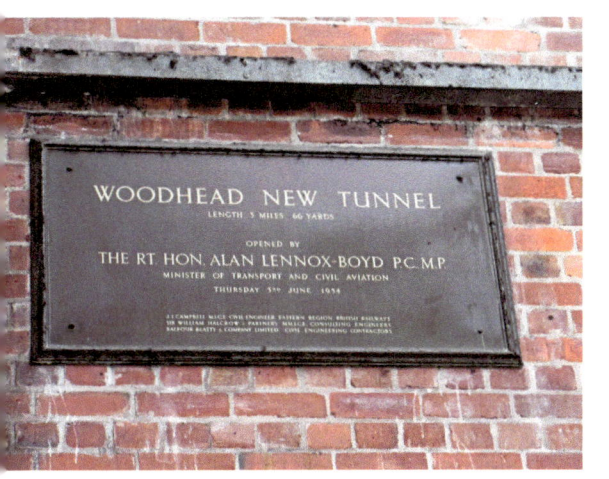

Above left: Commemorating Woodhead 3, this plaque at Platform 1 (originally Platform A), on the MS&L/GC side of Piccadilly, was unveiled in June 1954.

Above right: Date stone on the western (Woodhead) portal of Woodhead 3.

Right: EM1 No. 26054 hurries a heavy coal train away from Woodhead during the 'Rail Blue' period, 19 July 1972.

EM1, EM2 and EMU

The first electric locomotive for the route, No. 6701, designed by Sir Nigel Gresley and built by the LNER at Doncaster, appeared in 1941 – but had nowhere to operate and languished in store. It was a Bo + Bo locomotive with four traction motors, one per axle. With the end of the war, however, the opportunity was taken to loan the locomotive to the Dutch Railways, which were being reconstructed and electrified using 1,500-v DC overhead. No. 6701 started work in Holland in September 1947, working the Eindhoven–Utrecht Line. While in Dutch service, No. 6701 was nicknamed 'Tommy', which was subsequently formalised when nameplates – and a plaque commemorating its service on the Dutch Railway – were fitted. While in Holland *Tommy* had proved itself capable of hauling freight trains of up to 1,750 tons and had run half a million kilometres (or just over 62,000 miles).

Upon return to Britain, modifications were made to the production locomotives, which included: a larger, roomier cab; the up-rating of the steam-heat boiler (from 300 kw to 360 kw, and the water tank increased from 210 to 240 gallons) and the fitting of air-brakes and compressor. Freight-only EM1 locomotives had an iron weight in lieu of the train-heating boiler.

The EM1 was unusual in having no fewer than eight different braking systems:

– hand brake
– rheostatic
– regenerative
– train vacuum
– train air
– loco air
– driver's safety brake
– automatic air brake

The regenerative braking reversed the normal function of the traction motors, so that when the locomotive was not under powering, and descending a gradient under gravity, electricity was generated, which was fed back into the catenary, thus increasing the tractive resistance. It could be used when the traction motors were running series or parallel; when in parallel, regenerative braking could be used from 55 mph down to 30 mph and when changed over to series from 33 mph down to 16 mph, below which it was ineffective. The rheostatic braking system could then be engaged for speeds from 20 mph down to 4 mph.

There was also a weight transfer switch, which allowed the driver of an EM1 to weaken the field – and therefore tractive effort – in the leading traction motor of each bogey. This was in order to match the reduction in weight caused by the tilting of the bogeys during acceleration under power from a standing start to reduce the chances of wheel slip due to the locomotives having four-wheeled bogeys.

Power to the traction motors was controlled by electro-pneumatic contactors and resistances, and the ability to run in parallel or series led to a complicated driving technique:

> Initial acceleration must be at a restricted level of current, and is in series up to notch 15 (full field), after which greater speed can be obtained by changing to parallel and

Above: EM1 No. 260012, in BR Green, with a mixed freight in the 1960s.

Right: EM2 No. 27000 *Electra* stars in an advert for the British Westinghouse Brake Co.

Co-Co Locomotives for Manchester-Sheffield Line

Seven of these new locomotives, intended primarily for passenger service, and capable of a speed of 90 m.p.h. are now in service. The mechanical parts were built at the Gorton Works of British Railways, the electrical equipment being supplied by the Metropolitan-Vickers Electrical Co. Ltd.

Photo by courtesy British Railways Eastern Region.

are fitted with

WESTINGHOUSE

AIR-VACUUM BRAKE EQUIPMENT

by which the vacuum brakes on the train are controlled in synchronisation with air brakes on the locomotive by means of the Westinghouse vacuum-air proportional valve.
This equipment is similar to that on the Bo-Bo mixed traffic electric locomotives which have been operating on this line for some time.

Brakes made in England by
WESTINGHOUSE BRAKE & SIGNAL CO. LTD., 82 York Way, King's Cross, London, N.1

Representatives in India by **Saxby & Farmer (India) Ltd., Calcutta** *Representatives in Australia by* **Westinghouse Brake (Australasia) Pty. Ltd., Concord West, N.S.W**
Represented in South Africa by **Bellamy & Lambie, Johannesburg, Managing Agents for Westinghouse Brake & Signal Co. (S.A.) Pty. Ltd. Johannesburg.**

notching up again. A further four notches take the working into weak field in either series or parallel. It is rather a matter of experience which combination will give what result in any set of circumstance ...

In total this allowed for nineteen notches and two 'gears' (series or parallel).

Former Woodhead secondman Adrian Bailey remembered that dual-working, which was introduced in the late 1960s, was the 'biggest mistake' on the Wath–Penistone line. The locomotives had to be fitted with dual-brake systems, for which larger compressors were needed. It caused problems for the regenerative brake system but also when 'motoring' when heavy trains had to be worked up the Worsborough incline. If a train stalled when climbing the bank, re-starting the train had to be carefully coordinated; ultimately 'clear call' telephones were installed in the cabs, which operated via the overhead catenary wires.

In addition to the fifty-eight EM1s were seven large, EM2 Co + Co locomotives, built at Gorton Works and introduced 1953/54. The basic design was that of the EM1 but with six smaller traction motors. The power output in 'weak field' was increased from 1,868 hp of EM1 to 2,760 hp at 52.7 mph. The use of six rather than four traction motors permitted two stages of parallel and two stages of series working, giving three speed ranges. Numbered 27000 to 27006, the locomotives had a brief working life: they were used on passenger workings until 1968 when they were all withdrawn and sold to the Dutch Railways, becoming Nos 1501 to 1506; No. 27005 *Minerva* was scrapped for spares in 1969 in Dutch service. The decision to withdraw the entire class was due to the lowering of the speed

EM1s Nos 76016 and E26029 dual-working in the BR Blue era.

Class pioneer, No. 26000 *Tommy* at Manchester Piccadilly, resplendent in BR green.

EM2 No. 27003 *Diana*, pictured as No. 1501, at Eindhoven, 12 October 1985.

Class 506 M59046 at Glossop, July 1981.

M59403 at Platform 4, Manchester Piccadilly, waiting to depart for Hadfield. July 1981.

limit of the Woodhead Route from 65 mph down to 60 mph, making the faster EM2s surplus to requirements. Their death knell was the closure of Sheffield Victoria, ending the passenger service, in 1969. They were withdrawn from Dutch service in 1986 and three were preserved: No. 27000 / 1502 *Electra* at the Midland Railway Butterley; No. 27001/1505 *Ariadne* at the Museum of Science & Industry, Manchester; No. 27003/1501 *Diana* in the Netherlands.

For the local commuter services, eight three-car Class 506 Hadfield EMUs were built in 1950, having originally been ordered by the LNER back in 1938. They first entered service in June 1954. Each unit consisted of a driving motor brake third (seating fifty-two), a trailer composite (seating sixty-four, with twenty-four in first class and thirty-eight in third) and a driving trailer car (seating 60). The entire class was withdrawn in 1984 following the partial closure of the Woodhead Route and the conversion of the Manchester-Hadfield section to 25kv AC overhead operation. One member of the class was set aside for preservation but was ultimately scrapped in 1996. The Class 506 units were replaced by Class 303s transferred from the Glasgow area. The Manchester-Glossop/Hadfield trains are now operated by Class 323s, built by Hunslet Transportation Projects Ltd. in Leeds between 1992 and 1993. They were the last locomotives to be built at the historic Jack Lane works in Leeds, which closed in 1995.

Chapter 5

Working the Woodhead

Adrian Bailey began working at Gorton MPD as a locomotive cleaner in 1961 aged seventeen, with an 'ambition to become a train driver', and ended his career forty-seven years later (in 2008) as a station announcer at Manchester Piccadilly, after achieving his ambition to become a driver and doing a stint in the Control Office at Piccadilly. Today he is an active railway volunteer at the Museum of Science & Industry, Manchester.

Adrian began his career at Gorton Tank, on Cornwall Street: 'In those days you started at the bottom and worked your way up.'

EM1 No. 76025 at an anonymous classmate at Reddish depot in 1980.

I first heard about job vacancies through an uncle who was employed on the railway as a welder and platelayer. I was taken on as an engine cleaner. I reported to Gorton Tank depot, which was on Ashton Old Road (now Smithfield Market). I was issued overalls and then taken to the sheds where I was shown how to clean engines by ex-drivers who for health reasons could no longer drive trains. This involved lots of rags and wadding (the sort of stuff used in soft furnishings) and cleaning the side rods and eccentrics, smoke boxes door, numberplates and nameplates, engine cab backplates/face plates, cab floor and checking all the essential, i.e., brush, lamp, spanners, bucket, a box of detonators, which should include two red flags. Going with the Steam Riser who is there to show you how to light the fire and make sure you have enough water.

Having spent a few months as a cleaner I was then moved up to training as a fireman. This involved, initially, lighting up the boiler, loading the firebox with coal and lighting it with oily rags. You also had to fill the water tank and make sure there was enough coal in the tender for the journey ... Going with the Steam Riser who is an ex-driver doing Depot Work. The Steam Riser is there to show you how to light the fire and make sure you have enough water ...

I only had four months to get my fireman's ticket. You started as a Steam Riser and then went on to the 'Goon Link', covering for old drivers.

In 1965 Gorton Tank closed and he was transferred to Guide Bridge and from there to Newton Heath. With steam being phased out by 1968,

diesels came in, so firemen became secondmen (whose job was to assist the driver). Halfway through 1973 the title of secondman became redundant so I applied to become a driver. The test for this was a full day of Rules and Regulations. If you passed you could then become a driver after a few months' training.

Working as a fireman/secondman, in Adrian's opinion, was 'the best way to learn':

Gorton only had a small siding, for stabling of one locomotive. Most times the BoBos. At the time, Gorton Depot was the main operating depot, the manager was called Natmann, and a Mr Paine. Paine became duty manager at Store Street. Gorton Tank ran the engines at Ashburys, Gorton, Guide Bridge, Dinting. With electrification, motorman staff were a dual link at Gorton; Reddish Car Shops was the main fleet for the CoCos, and the occasional BoBo, for the passenger traffic. So that was for junior fireman who could move up the link to assistant motorman or secondman.

The signing-on procedure at Gorton was occasionally by telephone. If you were travelling to Reddish Car Shops, Guide Bridge or Mottram for work, you could book on by direct telephone from Gorton Station. In other word you didn't have the signing on and off duties like you had at a depot, where you had machines.

To get promotion on the BoBos and Cocos, you could move to Reddish, Guide Bridge or to Mottram Halt Siding. Reddish Car Shops, was passenger, Guide Bridge was freight and parcel traffic, and Mottram was trip jobs. But you could also go and work on steam at Dinting. Dinting had two steam engines. All those depots were run from Gorton Tank. A motorman could get more with travelling at Guide Bridge and also Mottram.

EM1s Nos 76021 (train engine) and 76008 dual working with a passenger train.

EM1 No. 76010 comes nose-to-nose with an unknown Class 40 at Guide Bridge, 20 July 1981.

Each depot had its own way of working. Gorton was very particular. Everything had to be spotlessly clean and was. If you came in on from the mainline on steam, and got over the wet pit, opposite Priory Signal Box, you had fire-droppers to do the disposal and drop the fire for you. If you wanted a tool, that was clean. Newton Heath was different. Jack of all trades really. Nothing was clean. If you went to prep and engine, you had to wash it all off with the slacker pipe first. What ever job you came off, you did all yourself. You had to drop the fire yourself – we had to take the firebars up, we had to be careful of the brick arch, unlike at Gorton where there was a fire dropper and a wet pit. Gorton Tank was a loco works and Depot, the engines we had on there were a mixture, 'PomPoms', 'Tinies', B1s, Derby1s, Derby 3s.

Cornwall Street was the main offices for the Depots. Cornwall Street is on Ashton Old Road. There's a road bridge, which goes over the top, just before you come to the station, not

75

the canal bridge, but before it. That came over Ashton Old Road, over Cornwall Street, to Hyde Old Road. Gorton Booking On for the Depot was on Malcolm Street. Malcolm Street went over by a road way cage to Beyer, Peacocks. It was a public way, but was a short way to get to Beyer, Peacocks.

Because Adrian was on a dual link at Gorton, he would often work steam as well as the Woodhead Electrics:

> Some of the [steam] Drivers were comical. They would *never* pass a water column without filling up, despite knowing where they were going. Other drivers in my early days were Rubin Valentine and Dick Kingston. If you was relieving a job at Preston, and the fire's going blue with clinker, because if you think about it, coming all the way down from Shap Summit, most if its down hill, so you're relieving men at Preston and you look round the fire and its blue. You know there's no air getting to that fire. There's two ways you could get round that: the Driver could notch it down, instead of winding it up, to mid-gear, to get some puff, to get that fire bouncing a bit; or you could use a long pricker, but you had to be careful because you were working under AC

EM2 No. 27003 *Diana* backing down on to her train at Sheffield Victoria, April 1964.

BR Standard 5MT No. 73069 having been released, *Diana* is coupled to her train of ex-Gresley LNER coaches to take the train forward to Manchester.

overhead. So a few firemen got killed doing that, never mind being caught in the wash-out pit. You had to be really careful. I remember a guy from Newton Heath going that way.

With the AC your limbs go to charcoal with the electricity. Your shoes melt. The stuff itself jumps up to three foot; it jumps even more in the wet. It's very dangerous stuff. DC current will throw you away from it; with the AC it pulled you toward it. I've never seen anyone electrocuted with the DC overhead, but with the AC, yes.

A locomotive firebox was also a handy way of disposing of unused detonators:

You used to get a tin of twelve detonators and two red flags, but they only last for so long. Some of the times when you go on they were out of date. So the idea was to get shut of some of them, so you can get a fresher pack of detonators. We just put them in the firebox.

There were other perks, too:

If you was on [Manchester] Victoria, the pilot engine, you'd single man it. Shovel in one hand, regulator in the other. Your mate would be back in the Staff Association Club beneath Victoria. You'd go out if someone wanted banking up Miles Platting, single man, and come back. You weren't meant to. It meant you got a social life. You went out whilst your mate supped and then would change over, so you could get a few in. Same with making extra money for the 'paper trains.' You'd stay and sort the papers. Victoria was really busy with the papers, all the paper were printed in Manchester at one time. You had Thomson House [now the Printworks entertainment venue], the *Express*, *Guardian*. All of them.

Promotion on the London Midland Region was quicker than that on the Eastern; so much so that it was hard to tell apart the driver and fireman/secondman on the LMR, while on the Eastern there was often a considerable age gap between the two. The best way to 'get on' was by initially taking trip workings from Mottram:

An EM1 working a passenger train at Torside in the BR green era.

The same location, around a decade later, in the BR corporate blue era.

You could get more from Guide Bridge or Mottram. Harry Churchill was the Traction Inspector; Terry Newton at Reddish Car Shops was another, but he became an alcoholic. I used to do his job, and he used to do mine, by sitting in the assistant's seat. You just had to make sure he was in the cab. Everyone looked after each other then. It was a case of going through the ranks. They were traction inspectors, and I had them as my drivers. Harry Churchill was one of my best drivers, he examined other drivers who were learning their jobs. So in other words, I had the best ones I could have. You got in the loop, in the link with them, and you do the job between you. You're not supposed to, but you did.

In that period, if you didn't smoke – always Castellas – or drink, you didn't get on. Most drivers smoke and drank. Every town, every city, had its own Staff Association Club. You could have a social life. It was like the start of the Night Clubs and, like Batley Varieties. And you'd go and have a drink and be seen. There were certain pubs which were only railway pubs. You go to lodging house, and get ready for coming back. At each station stop, you went back to the restaurant car and got six cakes and a tin of coffee or tea.

You could make eight [hours] into twelve, with overtime it was quite easy. Your supervisor [Driver] was with you all the time. You had some drivers who only wanted to do eight hours, they'd stay in the cabin and sup. But if they got to know you, and you wanted extra work, you got it. That's how you got on. Coming through the ranks, that was learning the job. You were the secondman, but a lot of the time the driver was in your seat. A lot of the time you worked the job between you. So at the same time you were learning rules and regulations.

After having signed on, the locomotive had to be prepared:

At preparation, you got to engine and got to the cab. Made sure the handbrake was on: nine times out of ten it usually was. You didn't need scotches. But you could usually tell if it was. To get the pantograph to go up, if there was insufficient air in the air tank, it's a matter of using a pump. The pump was in the corridor. So you got on and pumped it up. You could see, or your colleague could see, the pantograph rising. Once it touched the live wire, the compressor cut in and on your panel you've got a re-set button and you re-set that to get the pantograph to stay up. But if the pump wasn't working, you had to get something like those long wooden shop blind poles with a hook on the end, and clip it from underneath, and clip it onto the pantograph and hold it up to the wire until the compressor kicked in.

These engines could work from one or two pantographs and from batteries. You could only go where there was DC overhead. So in other words you have to be careful you didn't run off the wire. An alternative you could do, you've gone into the section, but there's no more wire, you could open the air cock, drop the pantograph and go on a bit. So instead of working on two pantographs, you were working on one. These engines were also capable of working on batteries. So if you were stuck on the mainline and the line dropped, and you know it's dropped by the gauges in the cab itself, the voltage has gone. You could coast like that.

They had a steam generator as well. We had to know about them, and they were a little bit different on the BoBo compared to the CoCo one. They worked A-OK. You had the water tanks underneath. If I remember, they had a little hot-plate and all. You didn't climb up to put water in it [for the steam heat boiler], there was a side valve. It was safer. It was only on diesels that you really had to climb up, for the train heating boilers.

You also had to set the lights. We was always trained to use the discs as well as the lights. So middle and right lights meant a fully fitted freight job. In other words, every vehicle in that train, as far as we knew, has got a braking system. If it had got middle and left, it would only be a partial train; if you've just got one in the middle, at the bottom, that's light engine. One over each buffer was an express train, like you do today. You had a red disc and a red lamp. That was always the procedure as far as tail lamps went.

EM1 No. 26046 running light engine at Woodhead station.

79

The EM1s and EM2s were famous for having eight different braking systems:

> The braking systems: you've got straight air, vacuum brakes, re-gen brake and a rheostat brake. So if you can't stop with that lot you've got a problem. The best one of the lot is probably, as far as controlling the *train* is concerned, is the re-gen and the rheostat. If you look in the cab on the CoCo, there's a switch in the middle. They decided later on for multiple working, but when I was on you could pull more or less anything with one engine, working on DC current.
>
> The best way of working was vacuum and just straight air. When they were made for tandem working, that's where the problems started. Because that's when one or two started having accidents. You didn't really require dual fitted stuff or tandem working really.
>
> The braking systems were great. The rheostat brake had three switches, B1, B2 and B3. You had to be quick at notching up, you came through the notches right up, right to the top, once you were going at high speed, notching up right the way round, and then you could start weak field. You had fifteen positions and could then switch to parallel and notch up again. On the controller you fetched it so far round, and once you got under fifteen miles per hour, without using brakes, you just turned B1, B2 and B3. So at the same time, what you're weighing up your line pole, on your panel. On the CoCo and BoBo you had a special lever, the reversing key, in the cab, and a dead-man's pedal, for forward and backward. If you had a fault in the ETH [Electric Train Heating] Room, where the actual fuses were – you never had to go in there really – you had to shut the engine down. You needed your engine key to release in the corridor, to get into the ETH Rooms, but you can't go in until the pantograph is down. There were air cocks in the corridor to bring down the pantograph. Just release them and the pantograph will drop down. There were knives on the top where you could isolate them; so you got that pole and you could isolate them with that. The battery switch was in the cab, and on the wall at the back of the cab.

Another task for the secondman was to 'hook up and shackle on':

> There were four platforms at Piccadilly, on the east side. We had to hook up and shackle on and pipe up. But if it went to the other side, the west side as they used to call it, they had a shunter to do it. A shunter at Piccadilly got crushed one year coupling up.

EM1 No. 76032 at Reddish depot in 1980.

Crew comfort was also superior to later diesel locomotives:

> The BoBos were quite easy locos to drive. There were two switches in the cab, exciter for the weak feed, and the coolers, the bellows, for the traction motors. There was no problem with them. The diesels were all different, which made for huge problems. You needed special training on each type of loco. We never called them 76s or 77s, always 25s and 26s. The BoBos were quiet, and pretty quiet in the cab. You had a nice desk; two nice seats and they weren't draughty, unlike the diesels. And the compressor wasn't that noisy, unlike some of the diesels ... There was a hot plate ... you could cook knife and fork on that ... On the 47s there was a hot plate at the number two end where the second man seat was. What you did, but you shouldn't have done, one of you would do the bacon and eggs whilst the other was driving. You did things like that then. Looked out for each other.

EM1 No. 76053 at Guide Bridge in 1980.

EM1 No. 76055 with two classmates at Guide Bridge, 1981.

Similarly, Ron Whitehead recalled that on his last turn on the Woodhead route

> I drove the train, Up to Rotherwood while the driver slept in my seat, on the way back I was sat in my seat and I noticed the driver was falling asleep, so I had to tell him to change places so I had to bring the coal train back, or there could have been a crash on my last turn. It was good that I had driven them a lot, in fact I had more experience on BoBos than that driver.

The EM1s had a tendency to bounce at speed, due to the use of leaf springs. On the EM2 this was overcome by having coil springs and six wheel bogeys:

> On a BoBo you could always feel the joint on the sixty-foot rail. You could always feel the mainframe and handbrake hitting the mainframe. The faster they went the more bouncy they got. On a CoCo they were pretty smooth. You couldn't feel the joints.

The EMUs were different again:

> These units used to come in different shapes and sizes. A lot of the ones we had were 'yellow diamonds', so if you got a 'yellow diamond' with a 'blue square' you couldn't connect them up! The EMUs were stabled at Ardwick; Ardwick 3 was a coach siding. We used to have a job on nights called the Staff Train, one an hour from Piccadilly to Mottram. We used to do the job between us; one would be in the cab, while the other would be on your back, asleep!

Adrian had little time for early forms of diesel-electric traction:

> They were building them all different, not standard, like with Brush-Sulzer with the Class 47s: fittings in the engine room could be different in one compared to the other. They had lots of different types. All these different type of traction, which meant schooling on each type and locomotive had be involved. Each Diesel had its own individual type of steam heat boiler. Class 25 boiler is what you call a baby stone engine; if you went to a Class 40 you have a large stone vapour engine, but the valves on them worked differently. On a 47 it might be a spanner boiler. Some coaches had steam generator boilers on then, not just from the engine.

Having prepared the locomotive, and backed onto the train and coupled up at Platform 1 at Piccadilly, the train was ready to depart:

> There were four platforms with a siding with DC current. We only had four platforms, the other side, one to twelve, were AC, and thirteen and fourteen at the time were DC, but then changed to AC. At Piccadilly, there was a stabling yard in the middle. Up line on one side, Down line on the other. Where the girder or the bridge is, sticking out now, was the siding. You could run in and out of it. We only ever had five or six bogeys on when working passenger services. One year, a train ran away through the blocks on Number Nine. Five and Six were the only platforms where you could run-round; the others were

Above left: EM1 No. 26033 with a westbound merry-go-round coal train, 19 July 1972.

Above right: EM2 No. 27003 *Diana* at Manchester Piccadilly, ready to depart with the 2.10 p.m. to Sheffield, 21 April 1964.

Below: EM1 No. 76027 and sisters at Reddish depot, New Years' Day, 1981.

all dead-end. You had to be careful coming down into Piccadilly. You would always be stopped at the signal. When coming into Piccadilly you were always tackled and had to stop and inform them what kind of engine you had, AC or DC.

We had no ship-to-shore radio in those days; we had to certify ourselves. If you passed a signal at Danger on the mainline, you just squared it with the Signalman. If you were on a goods line, you squared it with the tool van. If you'd past at danger, the Signalman knew you had, and you just sent the fireman back. There also used to be a lot of traps, if you went off at a trap you'd be half on your side. The catch points were all manned by Flag Staff, red and green flags in the day and red and green lights at night, *if* you could see them. You also had telephones, but could also send back tickertape.

Sidings were provided at Ardwick. There was a two-coach siding. You had an Up and Down fast, with a loop line to Piccadilly, and an Up and Down slow line for Ardwick 3. There was a depot at Ardwick 3, run by Gorton Tank. It consisted of a siding and also train crews. Steam Crews worked on steam in the sidings. In the sidings at Ardwick you went up to Ashburys, where there was a large siding for freight, with a junction for Midland Junction and Ancoats Siding. The only part which had overhead was to Midland Junction. There was a further yard at Priory Junction, the junction for Gorton Tank, part of Asbhury's Siding and also the Beyer, Peacock siding, and Gorton Works. It was most important because of the closure of the Belle Vue Depot in the 1950s.

At Fairfield Station there were six platforms; it was one of the only stations in our area with six. It wasn't just called Fairfield, but 'Fairfield for Droyslden'. There were two platforms for the Fallowfield Loop and four on the Sheffield side. It also had the junction for Hyde Road and down to Trafford Park, which passed the Reddish Car Shops. To get to Reddish Car Shops, there was a sharp right turn, where it passed over Hyde Road and down past the cemetery. So that part of the line was also wired. Reddish Car Shops was one of the few plants where they had a wheel-turning lathe. There were depots for the BoBos at Wath or Rotherwood and they came to Reddish Car Shops for repair. When you left Fairfield there was an Up and Down fast and an Up and Down slow. Just before Guide Bridge there was a railway bridge carrying a line over, which was from Denton Junction,

EM1s Nos 76046 and 76049 at Reddish, 1 January 1981.

and connected it to Droylsden Junction. This part has gone because of construction of the motorway. Droylsden Junction was like a shortcut really, a branch line.

Gorton–Fairfield was a triangle. It was ideal for the Reddish Car Shops. Because of that, the Midland Pullmans used to be based there, the Blue Pullmans were serviced there. So they went down the Fallowfield Loop. When you came out of Fairfield, there were remnants of a triangular junction, so when you came out of Fairfield you could've joined up with Ashton Moss, but it was never built.

There was one particular signal, just before Guide Bridge, where you could stop and stand for fifteen to twenty minutes on the Up slow Line. Not the fast line. If you'd got a freight train, nine times out of ten, you were going to Dewsnap Sidings, up the side of Guide Bridge.

At Guide Bridge were two sidings. On the left hand side, where the trains go into the station are the slow lines; the fast lines were on the other side, where it's all filled in. There was a signal box there. The actual Guide Bridge Station had a lay-by where if you had trains coming from Central Station, and we had them at Gorton, for Central Station toward Sheffield, they used to take the Steam Engine up the extremely steep bank from Throstle's Nest. The Locomotive stabled at Guide Bridge at the snicket would come out. The steam would come off and the electric go on. There was Cabin Side on one side, and the Liverpool Sidings on the other. They called it Liverpool Sidings because it was all downhill sidings from Woodhead. It was a matter of electric taken off and steam hooked on to take it forward from them. Later on, the electrics were stabled in Liverpool Sidings and a diesel tank installed at Cabin Side.

Class 25 No. 25196 inside Reddish Car Shops, 1 January 1981.

Dewsnap sidings were gravity-fed. So it worked by Shunter and also by Brake Staff, which were known as 'Brake Runners' – the Shunter would draw the train up out of the loop, weigh up the labels as to where the wagons were wanted, hook them off, and let them go down the sidings right to the blocks. Some of these shunters got hurt. They were swinging on these brake poles under their belly on the brake levers, and if it slips they're underneath. It was bit of a dangerous job really. Sometimes a Guard had to be very careful, because if he's preparing a train, on the block, he'll stay in his brake van, and if they haven't finished shunting a train which is come into the siding, and he's making his fire up, and doing his train preparation, he's got to be careful, that's its all right to go round it. There was also a ballast siding at Dewsnap as well as being a gravity feed.

EM1s Nos 26021 and 26041 running light engine at Crowden, 18 April 1964.

Eastbound tankers approaching Crowden, 13 August 1976.

E26048 in charge of an eastbound passenger working at Torside.

EM1 No. 26051 eastbound at Crowden with a mixed freight on 18 April 1964.

The road is still climbing, all the way, to Newton and Godley Junction. Godley had a large turntable. There was also a shunting siding, and trains coming up from Liverpool over the Cheshire Lines came up to Godley.

From Godley Junction you went through Hattersley to Broadbottom, and you crossed over the arches from Broadbottom Station. There used to be a way of getting in to the siding at Mottram Number One. There were two boxes, one at either end. These sidings were gravity-feed sidings again: don't forget, you're still climbing up and up. Mottram Yard had its own control Signal Box as well, in the sidings, in the middle. Mottram was for Trip Jobs. Coming out of Mottram and going to Ashton Moss, it was a very steep bank. It climbed to the right, but when you got more or less round it, it went down a dip, so if you had a train which was loose-linkered, you had to make sure you kept those shackles tight. Which is where the BoBos were really good. Ashton Moss Sidings were exchange sidings; it was virtually like a triangle, and you could go round to the left to Droylsden, Droyslden Junction, Denton and Miles Platting.

Dinting Junction was a triangle and a little Depot, where you went off to Glossop. It had a couple of roads, controlled by Gorton. If they were short-staffed, if you had sickness, they used Gorton men, who got an hour's travelling.

When you got to Hadfield, you were still climbing. And you had the arches at Dinting, which are of a considerable height and length. Before you went into Hadfield there was a loop line, on the left hand side. That loop was for any passenger traffic coming through; you went into the loop and let the passenger traffic pass. There was a 'box at Hadfield. There was also a 'box at Valehouse. When you came out of Hadfield, there was a bridge going over the top, it went straight and then went curve to the right where Valehouse was. At Torside, there was a box, and a crossing, and loops there, on the Up and the Down. The bank at Torside was dangerous, especially in winter with the snow. There used to be a cottage or two at Torside.

Crowden was quite a big station really, next to the reservoirs. On the hill opposite was quite a row of cottages. There was a loop between Crowden and Woodhead. And then you come to Woodhead Station. Woodhead Tunnel was one of the only tunnels which had modern lighting all the way through. Modern electric lighting, so it was always lit up in there. Compared to some of the tunnels which you get even today, like going to Liverpool Lime Street, it was like Blackpool illuminations in Woodhead.

When you got out at Dunford, there was a box on the left at Dunford Bridge Station. And it used to turn to the right. There was also a loop line, a loop on both sides, out and in. Bullhouses West box was on top of a little hill, it wasn't on the trackside really. Bullhouses was on the left hand side as you go into Penistone. It levelled out once you got out of Dunford, but when you got to Bullhouses it started to go down, down gradient. It went down and to the right and then turned to the left. Quite sharp and steep; it was quite nasty really.

There was a crossing at Shaw Hall, and there was a box on the left at Thurlstone Crossing. At Penistone there was Penistone Goods box on the left, and the goods yard was on the right hand side. There were two loops, one up, one down. Penistone Electric Control Station was the most important thing on the line. It was where all the AC to DC current was made. We never had the opportunity of going in. Penistone was a junction, a busy junction with big sidings. Part of the junction also went down the Wath Line. The actual Wath line was all subsidence, up hill and down dale. And this is where the DC

EM1 No. 26033 at Dunford Bridge in the early 1960s.

BoBo engines did well, because they were exceptionally good at controlling the freights trains up and down grade. Most of the freight trains went down to Wath Exchange, where they had large sidings as well for their BoBos. The actual junction went to the right, on to Sheffield. And then to the end of the line at Rotherwood Sidings. There was a works at Darnall, Cravens, where they built Underground stock.

It was all down gradient to Sheffield from Penistone, Wharncliffe, Woodburn, Hargreaves, Wadsley Bridge. Tinsley Yard was on the level, and only came in the end towards the end of the DC life really. The way the trains used to go in was via Ashburys, the Hope Valley, and Sheffield Midland. A lot of these modern yards, Tinsley, Healey Mills, Whitemoor, were all modern yards but built in the wrong era. A lot of the sidings were exchange sidings, for exchange purposes. You had a rack of vans on, or a rack of coal on. It was split out how it was wanted and a new engine would come on and take part of it on somewhere else. But it never materialised on the Woodhead. Perishable traffic from the east side of the country was to come to Ashburys, but it never materialised. We had a lot of traffic from Hull, coming from the Docks. Everything from the docks, a lot of continental van traffic, came into Ashburys. It was built in the wrong era. These modern freight yards never did their lifespan really. The idea was good for fast freight, but they were never used properly. It was a shame really.

Epilogue

The route had been full of potential when it was electrified, but the piecemeal nature of electrification and the hiatus caused by the Second World War meant, that by the time the line was completed, it was already obsolete as 25,000-v AC had been adopted as 'standard' in 1956. Following the Beeching Report of 1963, BR mooted proposals a year later to segregate freight and passenger services from Sheffield to Manchester: the Woodhead line was to be developed for express freight, while passenger services would go by the Hope Valley. Formal proposals were published three years later. A new yard at Tinsley had been opened in 1965; it was hailed at the time as a cornerstone in a new plan to revolutionise freight handling by rail. On 5 June 1967 BR announced its plans to cease passenger services on the Woodhead Route. The subsequent public outcry resulted in a two-year enquiry but, despite this, the Co+Co locomotives were withdrawn in 1968 and in August 1969 the transport minister gave his consent to withdraw passenger services. The last timetabled passenger train was to leave Manchester Piccadilly on 4 January 1970 at 9.20 p.m. but, because of a derailment at Valehouse, it was diverted via the Hope Valley Line. But the enthusiasts who had gathered to see off the last train had the last laugh: they held an impromptu 'sit-in' in the station manager's office. This resulted in a special train being laid on, drawn by No. 2605 *Pluto*, which departed at 11.10 p.m., reversing at Hadfield to avoid Valehouse, and running wrong line to Torside. It arrived in Sheffield at 12.44 a.m., bringing the curtain down on 125 years of passenger traffic through Longdendale and the Woodhead Tunnel.

The route was turned over to express freight. Freight, however, was on the decline during the 1970s and by the end of that decade BR was making noises about closure of the route. The line could have been re-wired to AC – as the present section to Hadfield and Glossop has been since 1983. The loss of trans-Pennine freight traffic, and the general decline in freight in general, made it logical to use spare capacity on the slower Hope Valley Line, which carries local as well as mainline services, rather than to invest in new equipment on the Woodhead Route. This was despite BR proudly stating that it was 'the most important line in the country'.

In 1980 BR announced its plan to close the Woodhead Route, believing it had a surplus of trans-Pennine routes, and the freight-only status of the line made it an easy target. BR, however, decided to maintain passenger services at each end, to be passed over to the

An unidentified EM1 at Reddish, January 1981.

EM1 No. 76057 lies rotting at Reddish depot, 1 January 1981.

Above and Below: The mortal remains of EM1s Nos 76057 and 76050 at Reddish, 1 January 1981.

Great Manchester and West Yorkshire Passenger Transport Executives. The rail union ASLEF estimated the cost to GMPTE for modernisation and conversion of their section of the route to AC at £300,000–500,000. ASLEF, however, were opposed to the closure of the route, stating that 'The Woodhead Route is not the first, nor the last line to be faced with a situation of declining demand.' Closure and reduction would mean the 'end of a strategic rail network' encompassing marshalling yards at Wath and Tinsley, which represented an 'unspecified' number of job losses. BR had estimated that conversion of the Woodhead Route to 25,000-v AC would cost some £24 million (ASLEF estimated the cost to be £200 million), and that, faced with declining freight traffic, this was an unjustifiable expense. ASLEF challenged this view, arguing that, while BR had published the estimated cost of electrifying Woodhead and considered it uneconomical, they were pushing ahead with electrifying the Diggle route, but had not published any costings. During March 1980 the issue of the closure of the route was raised in Parliament, with BR arguing in effect that the DC equipment was both obsolete and worn out, and that it was not economical to convert to AC. BR suggested that if traffic were to increase on the route, then it would be reprieved In May 1980. ASLEF was pushing for an independent enquiry into the proposed closure of the route.

The value of retaining the Woodhead Route was shown when on 6 February the Hope Valley Line was completely blocked and services diverted over the Woodhead, due to the derailment of a cement train at Earles Sidings near Hope. Later in the same month,

EM1 No. 76043 at Reddish, New Years' Day 1981.

on 22 February, a freight train was derailed at New Mills: it 'completely wrecked some ICI mineral wagons, and caused some hundreds of tons of limestone to fall down the embankment', blocking the freight lines. The usefulness of the Woodhead route was shown again at the end of the year when engineering work closed two tunnels on the Hope Valley Line on Sundays and all services were diverted via Woodhead until spring 1981.

The last train over the Woodhead Route, drawn by Nos 76006 and 76014, ran in the early hours of 18 July 1981, and the route passed into memory, and into myth. But while lines of EM1s stood rotting at Reddish and at Guide Bridge, Class 506 EMUs continued to trundle to Glossop and Hadfield, and new stations opened at Hattersley (1978), Flowery Field (1985) and Godley (1986). Operated by Arriva as part of the Northern Rail franchise, trains to Hadfield depart every half hour from Manchester Piccadilly; those to Glossop run with similar frequency, usually handled by three-car Class 323 EMUs. In December 2015 Arriva announced new rolling stock to supplement the 323s.

The route between Stalybridge, Guide Bridge and Piccadilly, built by the SA&M, is today used by TransPennine Express, heading all points east. The eastern route, from Penistone to Sheffield, remains open, carrying traffic from Huddersfield to Sheffield.

Ironically, in September 2016 Transport for the North announced there was insufficient capacity on existing TransPennine routes, especially for fast freight, arguing for a new strategic rail link between Manchester and Sheffield, as well as increasing frequency on existing routes. The report also highlighted the need for strategically placed Multimodal Distribution Parks, with good road, rail, and/or waterway links.

The Woodhead Railway Heritage Group was founded in spring 2016 to preserve and promote the history of the Woodhead Route. They have ambitious plans to open at Guide Bridge Station the Woodhead Railway Heritage Centre. This will be in time to mark the 175th anniversary of the opening of the first section of Sheffield, Asthon-under-Lyne, and Manchester Railway from London Road to Godley Toll Bar in December 2017.

EM1 No. 76002, still carrying a funeral wreath, 1 January 1981.

The end of the line at Hadfield, 13 August 2016.

Select Bibliography

Contemporary Newspapers and Journals including

Ashton Weekly Reporter
Manchester Courier
Manchester Guardian
Manchester Examiner & Times
Reynolds's Newspaper
Sheffield Independent
Sheffield Iris
The Illustrated London News
The Railway Magazine
The Railway Times
The Morning Post
Yorkshire Post
Yorkshire Evening Post

Printed Books and Pamphlets

T. Coleman, *The Railway Navvies* (London: Penguin, 1968).
G. Dow, *The First Railway between Manchester & Sheffield* (London: London & North Eastern Railway Co., 1945).
G. Dow, *The Third Woodhead Tunnel* (London: British Railways, 1954).
G. Dow, *The Great Central Railway*, vol. 1 (London: Ian Allen, 1985).
W. Harrison, *History of the Manchester Railways* (Manchester: 1882).
K. H. Vignoles, *Charles Blacker Vignoles: Romantic Engineer* (Cambridge: Cambridge University Press, 1982).